Arc·
to
Antarctic

To Sandra
with best wishes.

Mike Palmer

Mike Palmer

08. 10. 2011

CW00507398

First published 2011
© Mike Palmer 2011

MRM Associates Ltd
Reading, Berkshire RG1 7BX

ISBN 978-0-9569201-0-2

Photographs by the Author
unless otherwise stated

Produced through MRM Associates Ltd., Reading
Typeset by CJWT Solutions, St Helens
Printed in England

CONTENTS

Acknowledgements

I wish to thank the following people for their help in the preparation and writing of this book:

My Wife, Barbara, for her encouragement and support during this project; Dorothy Biggs (deceased) for being such an excellent landlady in my lodgings in Stanley; Warren Brown, www.browncreative.co.uk for much useful advice and assistance with diagrams; Dearle and Alma Draycott (deceased) for their hospitality to me in a far-flung corner of the British Empire! David Hewson, one time engineering officer on the *John Biscoe* for some excellent and useful photographs and advice; David Wheeler, my co-met-man at Grytviken during my time there, for his assistance and excellent photographs of whaling; Martin Marwood, MD, MRM Associates Ltd for guiding me through the technicalities of writing a book and its publication; Deborah Atsoparthis, for typing up the manuscript; Elizabeth Dill, for finding Countryside Books, through whom I contacted Martin Marwood; Dr Tim Hughes, for checking the contents of Chapter 9; Richard Wyatt, for permission to reproduce the article 'The Less Famous rescue plan for *SS Great Britain*'; Tansy Newman, Falkland Islands Government Archivist for researching correspondence in 1936 from the Governor, Sir Herbert Henniker-Heaton to the Mayor of Bristol, Albert Moon regarding the *SS Great Britain*; Giles Darkes, for copy-editing the book.

Introduction

The title of this book is taken from a letter written by a geologist friend of mine, David Broad, who worked on Somerset Island in the Canadian Arctic in the summer of 1966, when I was working in the Falklands.

A copy of the letter is shown below. The eradications and scribblings on it are interesting because they summarise the dispute between Argentina and Britain over the sovereignty of the Falklands. The letter was sent by David Broad, from Resolute, Somerset Island to Stanley in the 'Islas Malvinas' — his words! This was crossed out and 'Falkland Islands' written in its place, only to be angrily eradicated in the Buenos Aires PO and replaced by 'Argentina!' before it returned to the UK. When I finally received the letter, I reckoned that it had travelled around 16 000 miles, much to the credit of international postal services.

In Chapter 5, you will see the connection between this letter, and the events described in the chapter.

This book is dedicated to all those people who enjoy working in, and travelling through, exploring, or just visiting polar regions. It is not an exploration book, but it is a series of recollections and impressions of these high latitudes. I have tried to avoid too many facts and figures, except where I think that they help to illustrate the background to the writing. Facts and figures can be looked up elsewhere.

I have avoided speculation and politics as far as possible in my recollections, but in the last chapter *The foreseeable future of the polar regions*, I have taken on two controversial subjects, namely the dispute between Argentina and Britain over the future of the Falklands, and the increasing worries over the effect of global warming and economic exploitation of the polar regions, especially the Arctic Ocean.

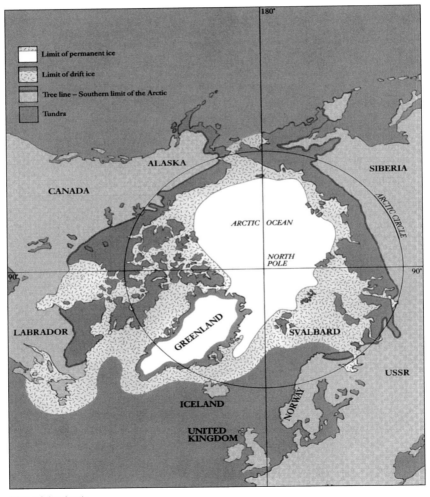

Map of the Arctic

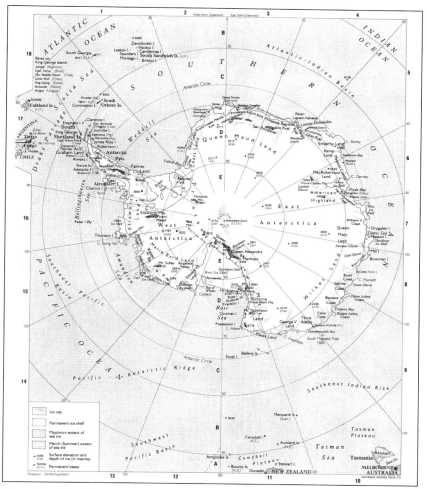

Map of the Antarctic

These regions are beautiful yet harsh, and challenging yet fascinating, as illustrated by the wonderful clarity of the air, the tremendous variety of colours and shapes of cloud, ice and sea, and the varied and fascinating wildlife and weather and peoples living there. Humanity must do its best to protect these places from the worst of changes and economic developments that will inevitably occur in the future.

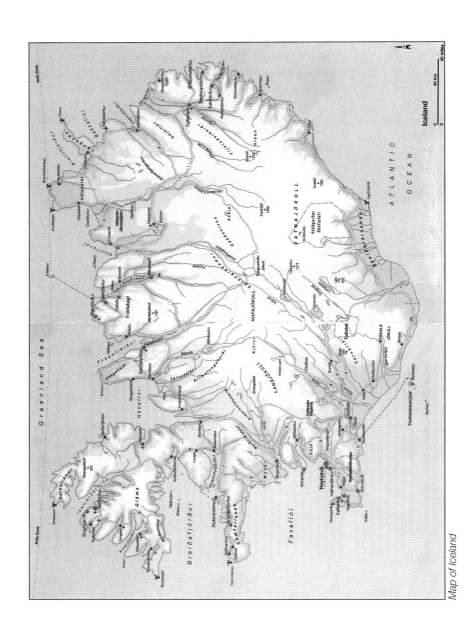

Map of Iceland

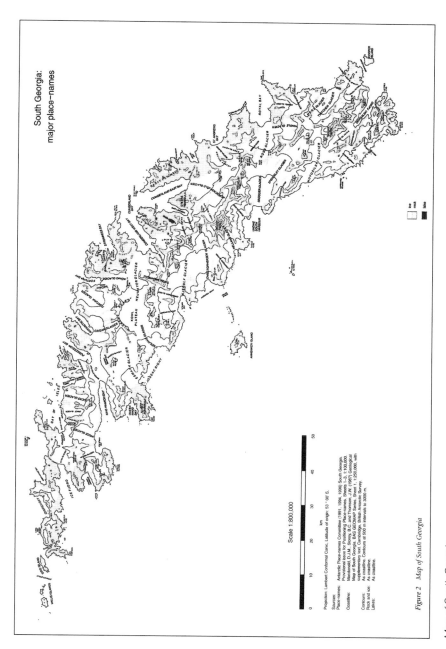

Figure 2 *Map of South Georgia*

Map of South Georgia

Map of Svalbard

CHAPTER 1

Background and Training

Using and repairing meteorological instruments

A s a boy I was always fascinated by cold weather and the polar regions. One of my earliest recollections is of being taken onto the Lake at Harrow School, where my father was teaching, during the icy winter of 1947. Soon I was reading of the exploits of the great Polar explorers: Amundsen, Shackleton, Scott, and Mawson, Nansen and Peary.

At the back of my mind was the desire to visit these places one day, but the question was how? My chance came when I obtained a place to study biology and chemistry at Hull University in 1963. At the Freshers' Fair I was asked to be Secretary of the Biological Society. I accepted, and was given a list of names to write to, including a Dr Martin Holdgate, then Head of the Biology Department of the British Antarctic Survey, based at Cambridge and London Universities. Dr Holdgate had been working and researching in Antarctica, especially at Signy Island in the South Orkney Islands. He agreed to give us a lecture about working in Antarctica and the prospects of working there. He advised me to get my degree then apply for a post, which I duly did.

So, having been appointed as a meteorologist/biologist, I began training at Stanmore in Middlesex. The training included instruction in operating and repairing the various meteorological instruments (including thermometers, sunshine recorders, anemometers and barometers) that we would find on the bases. These instruments included maximum and minimum thermometers from whose readings you can calculate the relative humidity, i.e. the amount of water vapour in the air. The warmer the air, the more moisture it can hold and this information is used to calculate the potential rainfall from clouds and air masses.

We also learned to use the anemometers which record wind speed and direction, sunshine recorders, and barographs which produce a trace on graph paper, thus showing a record of barometric pressure over a period of time (usually a week). We also practised using the rain gauges. Because of the extreme cold, precautions against the rain gauge freezing need to be taken, such as using a heat source close to the instrument.

The most interesting training experiences, however, centred around the pilot balloons which measured wind speed and direction at different heights. You filled a large red balloon with hydrogen gas, inserted a bung and released the balloon into the air. It ascended rapidly, and, using a theodolite, you tracked its elevation or angle of ascent and azimuth (in the form of a compass bearing) at one minute intervals, during which it ascended about 1000 feet. This allowed us to record wind speed and direction at height. I was astonished to find winds blowing at around 300 mph at 20 000 feet over Port Stanley — presumably jet streams. Filling these balloons was risky, and one day the hydrogen leaked out and ignited, due to static electricity, and one student became bald and eyebrowless very rapidly!

Before sailing to the Falklands we attended a pre-departure conference at Birmingham University. The highlight of the conference was the presence of Sir Vivian Fuchs, the then Director of the British Antarctic Survey. Sir Vivian led the Commonwealth Trans-Antarctic Expedition in 1957, during the International Geophysical year of 1957–58.

This expedition aimed to do what Shackleton had tried to do in 1914, i.e. to cross the Antarctic continent, via the South Pole. The expedition set out in November 1957, with six motor sledges, known as sno-cats, from near the Weddell Sea and reached the South Pole on 20th January 1958. It arrived at New Zealand's Scott Base on Ross Island on March 2nd, having covered 2158 miles in 99 days. This was a carefully planned expedition, using efficient and highly specialised machinery proving that such methods counted more than human endurance.

During the conference we were given lectures about life on the bases, how to deal with living in confined quarters for a long time, and safety, particularly when handling instruments in extreme cold, and when travelling across land ice (being aware of crevasses), and sea ice (being aware of melting, unstable, or thin ice).

I recall one startling photograph (alas, I do not have a copy of it!) of a FID (employee of the British Antarctic Survey) who urgently had to answer a call of nature while out on the ice, and who, unfortunately, became frozen to the ice by his private parts! I believe that the ice to which he had become attached was cut away and gently melted!

We were also warned about the dangers of wild life. Fur seals could be very aggressive if they had young and could give you a dangerous bite, and we were warned not to get between them and the sea. Leopard seals were another danger and have been known to attack small boats!

And finally, we were warned about the dangers of succumbing to the charms of the ladies of Montevideo, our first port of call, in Uruguay, South America. 'Do not,' we were told, 'put your private parts into places where most people would not put a broomstick' (not my words!). We had been warned!

CHAPTER 2

South to the Falklands

Life on board the *RRS Shackleton*

On October 6th 1965, my twenty-second birthday, in company with around 60 other young men — no women in those days — I sailed from Southampton, aboard the *RRS Shackleton*, bound for Montevideo in Uruguay, Port Stanley in the Falkland Islands and beyond, to the Great White South, home of the blizzard — and many adventures!

As I prepared to embark, I recall my mother asking 'are you really going all that way, in that little ship?' The *Shackleton* did indeed seem a little ship as she lay in the dock at low tide, but in fact was an extremely comfortable and well-built vessel, and very seaworthy, as I was to discover later in our voyage.

After leaving Southampton we 'Fids' — a nickname taken from the Falkland Island Dependencies Survey — settled into a routine of shipboard life which consisted mainly of eating, reading up about Antarctica and life on the bases, and helping with shipboard activities such as paint-scraping and repainting, cleaning and varnishing woodwork, and occasionally steering the ship. On one occasion, as the ship's head swung wildly to and fro, due to overcorrecting the helm, the Captain stormed up to the bridge, took one look around and said 'bloody Fids again' and disappeared below! I do recall being on the helm one stormy day with the bow pitching up and down alarmingly, making steering quite exciting! The trick was to never overcorrect … otherwise you went round in circles.

One of my specific jobs as a biologist was to record any insects or other wildlife in the insect-trap nets which were mounted in the rigging. As we proceeded southward, every morning at 10 a.m. local time I would haul these nets down, record and identify any insects caught in them, and enter the details in a special log. A few insects were caught daily, but there was nothing of much interest

The RRS Shackleton   (Photograph by David Hewson)

until one Sunday morning, when as usual I hauled down the trap nets, they seemed to sag rather a lot, and on emptying them out onto the deck, discovered to my astonishment several flying fish in them! Flying fish skim along the ocean surface, and occasionally land on deck, but never do they reach eighty feet up in the air. All was soon revealed however, when I heard several crew members giggling and laughing from a nearby doorway!

Our next excitement came when we crossed the equator. This was marked by the famous 'crossing the line' ceremony whereby the novices — first timers — have to pay homage to King Neptune. This involves reciting an article of homage to King Neptune, following by having to swallow a few mouthfuls of a foul concoction created by the ship's cook and the Chief Engineer, consisting, as far as I can recall, of a mixture of custard, vinegar, some form of engine oil, pepper and salt and gravy! Being such a foul concoction it caused violent spasms and vomiting so one was in need of a good hosing down by the crew, as seen in the photograph.

After about two weeks out from the UK we passed the rocky islands of St Paul's Rocks which rise a sheer 8000 feet from the sea bed. Soon after this, the engine was stopped for repairs, so it was 'hands to bathe'. Now, swimming in a pool or off a beach is one thing, it's warm and you can usually see the bottom and there are no sharks; but here, a few feet down the water was cold and increasingly dark, so that if you dived and looked down, you got a weird feeling — akin to vertigo (after all it was an 8000 feet watery void beneath) — and there were sharks about, but the crew kept watch from the ship's launch.

As cats have their proverbial nine lives, I suppose we humans have a few spare lives — in the form of near misses. My first life was used up one evening, during a drinking session in the crew's mess. Whether as a joke or intended to impress me with his prowess at darts, a crewman threw a dart towards me: it thudded into the panelling about one inch to the right of my head, at eye level!

And so, in late October we arrived in Montevideo, the capital of Uruguay. This city was quite surprising in several ways, it seemed very American, most people being dressed in check shirts and jeans, and the streets were teeming with traffic, mainly elderly Fords, Buicks and Chevrolets which seemed to be everywhere.

It seemed that among the crew, a visit to the fleshpots of Montevideo was de rigeur and they were only too keen to initiate us Fids into the delights of downtown Montevideo! We also visited a lovely old restaurant called the Cafe Annacapri where we were entertained for several hours after our meal by a quite extraordinary blind harpist. I had never, ever heard such music in my life and was completely entranced by his playing.

After leaving Montevideo, we settled down again to shipboard life: But soon one noticed a marked difference in the air. The sea became a deep blue, and with gusty headwinds the waves became longer and more frequent. The air became cooler and soon thick jumpers and coats appeared.

Just after midday on our fifth day out, word went around that the Falklands could be seen ahead, and indeed the peak of Mount

Insect trap nets. These are mounted in the rigging to trap insects to indicate their movements.

Launching a radio-sonde balloon, to measure pressure, temperature, humidity and upper atmospheric winds. © The Met Office.

Reading thermometers at a Stevenson screen.
© The Met Office.

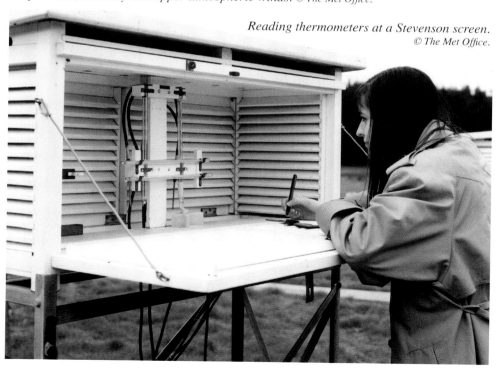

F.I.D.S departing Southampton, Oct 1965.
Sir Vivian Fuchs 5th from Left, author 3rd from left.

Preparing for the ceremony of 'crossing the line', paying homage to King Neptune.

A F.I.D. being washed down after crossing the line.

Flying fish on the deck.

Dolphins in the bow wave.

First view of Port Stanley, showing the cathedral.

Remembrance Day 1965. Note governor, Sir Cosmo Haskard in plumed hat.

Fox bay, a typical camp farm.

Mutton carcasses, also known as '365', being loaded aboard RMS Darwin.

The lopez family from Uruguay and Hugh Waldron, Anglo-Argentinean rancher.

The Lady Elizabeth.

The Fennia. Four masted Finnish barque, used as a wool store by the F.I.C.

The Fennia under sail.

Launching the Great Britain, July 1843.

Bow view of the Great Britain.

Stern view of the Great Britain.

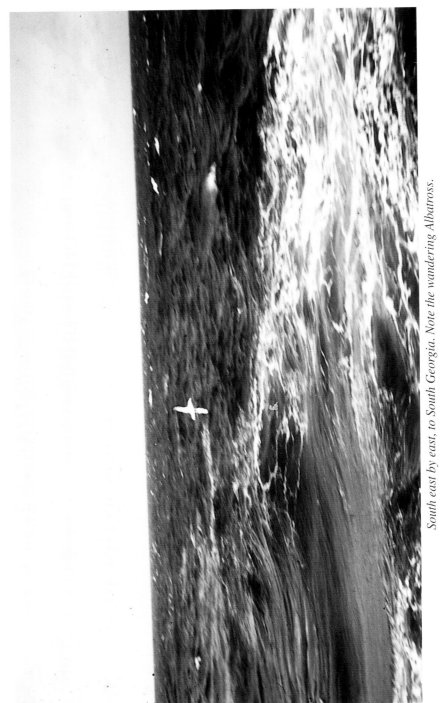

South east by east, to South Georgia. Note the wandering Albatross.

Kent slowly appeared above the horizon, followed soon by an extraordinary and pungent smell drifting across the water: peat smoke and seaweed. So evocative is the 'sweet-sour' smell of peat smoke that whenever I smell it, I am instantly reminded of the Falklands.

And so, after a voyage of approximately three weeks, we had arrived at our destination: Port Stanley. This then was to be my home for the next two months until my departure for that most spectacular of Antarctic islands, South Georgia.

CHAPTER 3

Arrival at Port Stanley

Life and work in the Falklands

M y first impression of the Falkland Islands was the wind. It gusts, roars, rips and tears at you continuously. Often there are two full gales a week, so the wind really is the determining feature of the weather here.

However, despite the wind (or perhaps because of it), the Falklands are a meteorologist's paradise, with a constant parade of ever-changing clouds passing overhead, from nimbus to cumulonimbus, altostratus to cirrus, all moving quickly on the winds aloft. Quick changes of cloud lead to an endless succession of rain, hail, heavy thundery downpours, all intermingled with brilliant, even breathtakingly bright, sunshine. The rapidly changing weather reflects the continuous procession of depressions moving from west to east, with their associated fronts. This constant meteorological parade passes overhead two or three times a week, so a calm day is a rarity there, with never a dull moment, meteorologically speaking.

I lived on board the *RRS Shackleton* for a few days after arrival, and it was during this time that I used up a second life. The ship was moored to bollards on the town jetty by four large ropes or hawsers, from the bow to the stern. A pal of mine and I decided to crawl along these hawsers from the jetty to the bow for a dare! As we proceeded the hawsers sagged, lowering us into the seawater, which at about 8°C (46°F) was not a pleasant experience, and furthermore, as I tried to extricate myself, I was caught up in vast fronds of kelp that seemed to have a life of its own entangling my legs and pulling me further down into the icy water. Lesson learnt: don't fall into the kelp beds, you could drown quite easily! The kelp seaweed incidentally, gives the Falkland islanders their nickname of 'Kelpers', so if ever you're invited by a kelper for a 'smoko, in the camp', you will be going to have a cup of tea with a Falkland islander in the countryside!

After a week or so I went to work as an observer at the Stanley Met Office up the hill and to the south-east of the town. We observers worked 12-hour shifts, the worst one being through the night from 4 p.m. until 4 a.m.. The work consisted of taking readings from the meteorological instruments once every three hours. The readings we took included from thermometers (wet and dry bulb thermometers to calculate the relative humidity), barometers and barographs for air pressure, an anemometer for wind speed and direction, a rain gauge, and a sunshine recorder. We then converted the readings into five-figure codes which were given to the duty radio operator to send to London and the World Meteorological Organisation in Geneva.

We also had to record cloud types and heights — here are some examples:

Clouds Low, CL	Stratus, nimbostratus and cumulus, between ground level and 10 000 feet
Clouds Medium, CM	Altostratus and altocumulus, between 10 and 20 000 feet
Clouds High, CH	Cirrostratus, cirrocumulus and cirrus, between 20 and 40 000 feet

We also recorded the amount of sky covered by each cloud layer, in tenths of the sky. If you look carefully at the sky you will see that it is rarely totally cloudless. An example might be 3/10 covered in cumulus cloud, 5/10 in altocumulus, and 2/10 in cirrus on a fine day, with a few showers and approaching wet weather indicated by the cirrus.

We also took pilot balloon readings, as described in Chapter 1, and radiosonde balloons were used as well, although I did not launch them myself.

Another vital job was to record the 'QNH'. QNH is a Q or question code. This abbreviation dates from the days of Morse code, when many of the questions most commonly asked by pilots were incorporated as code abbreviations in order to avoid long Morse signals. The letters QNH meant 'Question, no height' and is a request for atmospheric pressure at sea level, which is then used to set an aircraft's altimeter. So an aircraft's altimeter setting will depend upon barometric pressure at sea or ground level as applicable.

An additional task at the Stanley Met Office was to read out the daily weather forecast, including the QNH settings, for the Otter seaplanes which flew around the islands in those days.

By now I had settled into a routine, living in a comfortable British Antarctic Survey lodging house, at 5, Crozier Place, which I shared with two other men, both radio operators. Our landlady, Dorothy Biggs, looked after us three blokes very well, providing an amazing range of stews, casseroles, soups, mince, and chops, all based on the ubiquitous '365' or mutton, from the islands' vast sheep flocks. Our diet was basic country cooking, filling and nourishing with most ingredients being home or locally produced. Beef from the wild cattle herds, was an occasional and delicious change, while fish was available on Fridays, although I was surprised to see how little fishing took place around the islands.

Two other foods were major items of our diet. The first was delicious bread baked in the oven of the peat-burning stove — Dorothy complained that she could not keep up with our bread consumption — but we fell on it! The other staple was eggs. These had the reddest yolks that I had ever eaten, due to the chickens or 'chooks' being mainly fed on discarded sheep bones!

The lodging house was always warm and comfortable due to the magnificent peat-burning stove, now sadly replaced by an oil-fired central heating boiler — less cosy, but no riddling at dawn needed!

Before I left the UK to travel to Stanley, I had been given the names and address of the then headmaster of Stanley School and his wife — Dearle and Alma Draycott. I soon contacted them, and they invited me to their house on several occasions and were most hospitable. One day they invited me to join them in 'peat wriggling'. I imagined that this was some form of Falkland Islands ritual or game, possibly involving sheep. But no, this was hard, wet, cold work! It involved cutting and stacking blocks of peat, putting them into small pyramidal piles which were dried by the wind (plenty of that) and sun. Most residents in those days rented a peat bog from the Islands' Government to provide a cheap fuel. When I returned to the Falklands in 2004, I detected very little peat being burnt. I think central-heating oil has largely replaced it.

Christmas 1965 was now approaching and it can be a lonely time for someone on their own, so far from home, so the Draycotts kindly invited me to join them for Christmas Eve drinks, along with a teacher from the Camp who was staying with them.

And so, another of my nine lives came to be used up! Little did I realise the effect of a few bottles of beer, some Chilean wine, and two — yes two — bottles of Bacardi, consumed by three of us in about as many hours, would have! I do recall staggering back to my digs along Ross Road about midnight, the street lights seemed to be crazily zigzagging around, then a fall down some steps onto the beach. Luckily the tide was out — my third life! About 36 hours later, I crawled out of bed, still feeling grim and vowing never to repeat the experience! I never have.

Stanley celebrated New Year's Eve with a fancy-dress Ball in the Town Hall, to which I recall going as a tussock clump. Tussock grass grows in clumps about eight to ten feet high in ungrazed areas around the coastline. So I was enclosed in this grass tube, with a wide belt around my waist, the arrangement looking quite effective until I tried to do the conga, when to my embarrassment, I left a trail of tussock grass shoots all across the dance floor!

On New Year's Day Stanley races were held on the race course to the west of the Town. This is when the 'Camp' comes to Town. The Camp is a word derived from the Spanish word *el campo* meaning the countryside. It's a very jolly occasion, with horse racing, athletics, and a tug-of-war — often won by naval crews from any visiting warship — which in those days was, I recall, *HMS Protector*.

The overall impression of life in the Falklands in those days was one of self-sufficiency and 'make do and mend', hard work and adaptability in a difficult, almost frontier-like land. Although there was a slight friction between the islanders and people who came in to run various organisations, I personally found them very helpful and friendly, once you got to know them. However there was always a distant shadow hanging over the islands, of which we all became aware in April 1982.

Just as I was settling into a routine, my life changed dramatically. I was offered the chance to work in Grytviken on the magnificent island of South Georgia for the remainder of the Austral summer and autumn. And so, at long last, I set sail aboard the *RRS John Biscoe*: destination Gritviken, South Georgia.

CHAPTER 4

On to South Georgia —

the Gateway to Antarctica

So far, in this account, I have resisted giving you, dear reader, lots of facts and figures. They can be found elsewhere and can be very boring. However South Georgia is a unique island, so some facts and figures by way of introduction may be relevant. The island lies about 900 nautical miles south-east of the Falkland Islands between 54° and 55° South and 35° to 38° West. It is a crescent-shaped rocky island, dominated by the Allardyce Range whose highest point, Mount Paget, is 2934m ASL. This was often visible from my window in Shackleton House, and provided a wonderful backdrop. There are many deep inlets, bays and fiords which provide shelter for its magnificent populations of King Penguins, skuas, Adelie Penguins, albatrosses, elephant seals and various whale species. The island was first sighted in 1675 by Antoine de la Roché, a London merchant, but it was explored and claimed for King George III by Captain Cook in 1775. It was the centre of a vast whaling industry until the 1960s when the industry collapsed due to uncontrolled exploitation.

I travelled to South Georgia on the *RRS John Biscoe*, a sturdy, tough, ice-strengthened supply ship. She was less comfortable than the *RRS Shackleton*, and this was not a pleasure cruise!

On arrival in early January 1966 at King Edward Point, I was given a room in Shackleton House (now demolished) and allocated to my duties in the met office there. There were three met men: a senior met officer and two assistants, David Wheeler and me. David Wheeler and I became good friends, and he showed me a lot of the locality, and we had a few adventures together. Oddly enough I was to contact him again 40 years later in 2008, still living the island life, on Fair Isle when he appeared on the television programme *Coast*.

Our routine was much as before in Stanley, 12 hours on, 12 hours off, but we had enough free time to explore the locality.

The RRS John Biscoe   (Photograph by David Hewson)

South Georgia lies within the line of Antarctic convergence, now called the polar frontal zone. This is an area of cold north-east-flowing Antarctic water that sinks beneath warmer, less dense subantarctic water. Across this zone, the water drops 2–3°C in temperature, while salinity and dissolved oxygen levels also change. The island's wildlife, fisheries and weather are heavily influenced by its position to the south of the polar frontal zone.

During the late summer to early winter (January to April), the weather can be quite variable, ranging from raging blizzards, to mild sunny days and to the hot blast of a föhn wind. On one occasion, during the night a blizzard arose. At home in England, blizzards are a great inconvenience, and possibly dangerous, but in Antarctica, they can rapidly become lethal. Violent gusts, blinding spindrift and fiercely low temperatures, made worse by the wind-chill effect and disorientation, have led to several deaths in Antarctica. One way to combat this is to provide a lifeline from the met hut to the instruments in the Stevenson Screen, and one can follow it there and back.

On this occasion, a pitch-black night, with a howling gale and blinding snow, I set out to read the instruments. Suddenly, about halfway out I crashed into what felt like an enormous rubbery slug — only this slug reared up in the dark with a tremendous gerumphing, spluttering and hissing, and knocking me to the ground! For a second or two I was quite stunned, then realization dawned upon me: I had stumbled into a dozing elephant seal!

Sometimes the weather was wonderful — crystal clear and cold, but sunny. Most days however were cool at 5–8°C (46°F), showery, often with snow showers, and windy, with night frosts. However, one evening we experienced an extraordinary weather phenomenon: a föhn wind. It was a relatively mild evening with evening sunlight backlighting the mountains. Slowly I became aware of a rising westerly wind, but it was a warm wind. It rapidly increased to gale force, the temperature shot up to about 20°C (72°F) and water began to cascade off the local mountains, from rapidly thawing snow and ice. From the direction of the Allardyce Range came deep rumbling and crashing sounds as avalanches slid down the steep slopes — this was a föhn wind, much feared in the Swiss Alps as a cause of tremendous avalanches.

It occurs when warm, moist air from a certain direction (the west in our case) rises rapidly over the mountain and then cools, moisture condenses out as rain or snow and the air dries out. It then descends rapidly in the lee of the mountains and becomes compressed as it sinks to sea level and thereby heats up, just as pumping air into a bicycle tyre heats it up. So it is now a warm, even hot, dry wind and it races through the valleys melting all before it. However it only lasts three or four hours before fading away. An uncanny experience!

Another interesting aspect of working in the met office were the magnificent cloud formations, most notably pillow and lens clouds. One evening a clump of these had formed to the east of the base, and there were backlit by the setting sun, giving a 'Chinese lantern' effect.

Lens clouds are 'orographic' clouds and form when air is forced upwards as it passes over a hill or mountain. As air rises, it expands, and cools. The water vapour molecules join up to form condensation, seen as clouds. Their shape occurs when the air stream adopts a wave-like motion in the lee of a summit. The air blows through the cloud, droplets form at the front of the crest, then evaporate again at the rear of the crest, so the clouds appears stationary, although the air is moving through it.

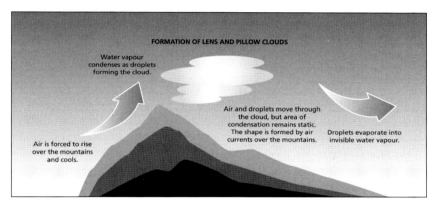

FORMATION OF LENS AND PILLOW CLOUDS

Water vapour condenses as droplets forming the cloud.

Air and droplets move through the cloud, but area of condensation remains static. The shape is formed by air currents over the mountains.

Droplets evaporate into invisible water vapour.

Air is forced to rise over the mountains and cools.

Diagram by Warren Brown

When our off-duty days coincided, David Wheeler and I explored the locality and it was during one of these explorations that I used up my fourth life. We had walked up beside a small cirque glacier to the ridge above it, behind Gryviken. A cirque glacier is one that forms in a bowl or valley head, on a mountain, as opposed to a glacier that flows down from an ice sheet. On reaching the top of the glacier, we decided to take a short cut across it, rather than walk around the ledge.

After about ten yards across it, David suddenly shouted 'Stop! Stop!' Then I realised that the whole area of snow was shuddering and slowly sliding downwards! Then it ceased to move. 'Make your way back to the ridge' David said, and we did so, having narrowly escaped triggering an avalanche — that was so scary!

Other walks included such exciting activities as scree running (running and bouncing down steep scree slopes, moving on before the scree begins to move), and swimming in the reservoir above the whale factory, to wash off all the dust —great, but there were icebergs floating in it!

We also explored the Lyell glacier which entered the sea in

Cumberland West Bay, and we walked over the Hestesletten Plain, to look at the ice fall from the Hamburg glacier. Here blocks of ice as big as houses would tumble over a rocky ledge, cascade down the slope and reform as a glacier on the plain below. This trek involved wading through an icy river three feet deep, socks and trousers off, boots on to protect our feet. During our walks we would encounter the local wildlife: a large Gentoo Penguin colony, which had, however, been decimated by some Japanese sailors from a whale factory ship — why?

One afternoon while walking out to Maiviken harbour something struck me a vicious but glancing blow on the head. Looking up I saw a skua approaching for its second attack — obviously I was in its territory!

The elephant seals on the southern side of Kind Edward Cove provided us with some amusement. Since they lay along the beach at right angles to the sea, it was possible to run up to them, jump on to the first one and bounce all the way along the row waking them up, and causing them to inflate their proboscises and to rear up into the air, while exhaling large amount of noxious gases. Their breath stank!

We had a resident King Penguin, who was tame enough to be fed by BAS staff, and who one evening was kidnapped, put in someone's room and left alone. He objected to this treatment by shitting everywhere, and when the culprits owned up (after a few beers) they had to clean the mess up!

Base life was comfortable; we were well fed by the catering staff, who can be seen catching dinner in the photograph. Meals were well prepared and substantial, suited to a cold climate. During my time there, I got to know the maintenance staff at the old Grytviken whaling factory, and I was shown round the buildings. People who have worked in South Georgia will remember the 'Kino', cinema and the church (now dedicated as a memorial to the life of Sir Ernest Shackleton) and possibly the manager's house which is now a fascinating museum of whaling, brim full of whaling memorabilia.

I was also shown the brass vats in which whale blubber was rendered down. I recall that there were about 50 vats in each shed, at least three sheds, so 150 vats. This brass was the scrap metal that attracted the Argentine scrap metal merchants in 1981. The brass in these vats must have been worth a fortune.

Finally, a look at the industry for which South Georgia was so infamous — whaling. This industry was established in 1904, by the Norwegian C.A. Larsen. It was very successful and led to the establishment of six whaling stations on the Island by 1912–1913. Most companies operated by using whale catchers from shore stations, but some used factory ships anchored inshore with land-based facilities. The factory ships operated at sea; they were supplied with whales, harpooned by the whale catchers, and processed the whale meat on board. These were the pelagic factory ships.

The shore-based industry declined from the early 1930s due to the scarcity of whales around South Georgia and the use of pelagic factory ships. Operations ceased in 1965, the year before I arrived. However, my co-met man David Wheeler gave me some excellent photos which he had taken in 1964. Whales were caught by harpoons fired from the bow of a whale catcher, a small trawler-like vessel, marked with flags and towed into the factories, hauled up onto a platform where they were cut up to remove the blubber — a process called 'flensing'. The blubber was melted down in the brass vats to produce whale oil, the bones were ground into bone meal and the flesh used for whale meat. The guts were cooked and used for animal feed, and a waxy material called ambergris was extracted from the head to be used in perfume making. Nothing was wasted but it was a dangerous, bloody and grim business, now largely ceased, but still carried on in a small way by whalers from Iceland, Norway and Japan. Many seals, especially elephant seals, were also hunted but whaling yielded much greater financial rewards.

And so, in April 1966, my time in South Georgia was over, and not until 2004 when I returned on an Antarctic cruise ship the *Akademik Ioffe* was I to see that magnificent island again.

On my return to Stanley, I settled down to life in the met office and the town, which was rather dull after the glories of South Georgia. However, in June of 1966 I was able to take a week's local leave which I used to travel around the islands as a passenger on the *RMS Darwin*, the Islands' supply ship. The ship called at several of the camp settlements including Darwin, Fox Bay, and Port Howard, dropping off supplies and collecting sheep carcasses and wool for export.

An interesting incident occurred one morning as we sailed through Falkland Sound. Just as I was having a 'smoko' and cup of tea about 11, there was a violent jolt, and the steward turned to me and said, 'that will be another one to mark on the chart!' such was the state of navigational charts around the Islands at that time!

I also met a gentleman called Hugh Waldron, who was travelling around the camp stations and who was an Anglo-Argentine rancher. He explained to me that he could not live on his *estancia* in Argentina for more than six months at a time, because he would be called up for National Service, so every five months or so he came to live in the Falklands again.

And so, in August 1966, I flew back to Britain after an adventurous and fascinating year in a remote part of the world that few people knew much about until the events of April 1982 brought it into prominence. However, I do recall people in Stanley saying to me, 'one day the Argies will get this place you know'. How right they were to be concerned. The next chapter relates a little-known and unforeseen incident which helped to confirm their fears.

CHAPTER 5

Invasion 1966

Argentine patriots hijack an aircraft
and force it to land near Stanley

In late September 1966, a group of 20 Argentinean nationalists
calling themselves the Condors hijacked an Aerolinas Argentinas
DC4 on an internal flight from Buenos Aires to Ushuaia and
forced it to land on the racecourse. The following account was
broadcast by the Falkland Islands' Government to inform people,
especially those in the camp, of developments, as they occurred, on
a daily basis.

*A broadcast talk on the token invasion of the Falkland Islands by
Argentine citizens*

'I am going to try and give you a general summary of the events
of the past two days, mainly for camp information — I think most
of us in Stanley are fairly well briefed.

'Yesterday, Wednesday, was quite a nice morning and we saw the
sun for the first time for several weeks — there was a little low
cloud. We heard reports from the camp that an Argentine airliner
had been seen flying overhead. This, of course, occurs regularly in
the winter and nobody took very much notice until about 9.40 *a.m.*
— we thought then that the Beavers had taken off very early
indeed, but did not think it looked quite like flying weather yet.

'Looking out we saw a four-engined plane, flying over Stanley
from west to east. There was no cloud and the aircraft was fairly
low. I thought, at the time, "I hope they know there are some new
masts up to the west of the town" because I do not think the red
lights on their tops are alight yet. Anyway, the plane turned round
and came along above Ross Road with the wheels down, skimmed
the cathedral and it was obvious that a landing was going to be
attempted — with such a large aircraft this did not seem possible.
There was a terrific scurry in town and I should think that every

land rover was moving along Ross Road towards the west. I suspect that the 20 mph speed limit was exceeded in some cases.

'By the time we reached the race-course there was an Aerolinas Argentinas DC4 plane bedded down there. Her number is LV-AGG and men were disembarking. A large crowd of people started walking through, from where Dorrans are building the new houses, towards the race-course and then we noticed that these men, from the plane, were wearing anoraks (rather like those worn by the Marines). They were waving rifles round and shouting to us to get back. One or two of the first people on the scene, including Police-Sergeant Peck, went up to them quite naturally and were promptly herded into the aircraft at gun-point. In fact, a total of some 20 people were taken inside in the first instance. Very shortly it was obvious that these men had come here in a demonstration and they had to be cordoned off by our own security troops. The Marines, the Police and, as soon as they could be mustered, the Defence Force took up positions round the plane.

'Meanwhile, traffic was stopped from coming further westward than Sullivan House, and three members of the rebels, who had taken over the plane, were brought down to be interviewed by the Acting Governor, Mr. L. Gleadell. One of them is a blonde, quite young, and she appears to be one of the leaders. They advised Mr. Gleadell that they had come to regularise the position of the Falkland Islands in view of the Argentine claim and that they felt they had as much right here as anyone else. They were told that they must immediately disarm and give themselves up for judgment. They were allowed to return to the plane as there were some 20 Falkland Islanders being held as hostages. In addition to the party, which we later discovered numbered 20, there were some 26 other passengers, including 5 or 6 women and a number of children. The youngest, I hear, is about one year old and, quite obviously, no action could be taken that would endanger innocent people.

'We found out later that this plane had taken off from Buenos Aires at about 12.20 a.m. yesterday — that is the 28th — and was flying a normal commercial service to Rio Gallegos. When the plane was in sight of Rio Gallegos these members in the passenger cabin — members of a group known apparently as the Condor Group — rose from their seats. They all had little bags with them and they took out anoraks, put them on, locked up the steward in the lavatory, broke into the baggage compartment and secured their rifles. They then went forward, telling the passengers to keep quiet. Four of them threatened the pilot and other people up in the front of the plane, telling them they must obey orders and make for the Falkland Islands. Apparently they had some idea that there is a landing strip or landing field here, and they spent a lot of time flying round looking for it. In the end the Captain pointed out that he had fuel for only 30 minutes and would have to put down somewhere. He considered landing on the sands at York Bay, or a belly landing in the harbour. I am very glad he did not do the latter because it was a cold day and it would have been a job to get boats out to the aircraft in time to save the people. Finally he decided to land on the race-course. He came in and appreciated, I think, that it was fairly soft — it is very soft at the moment — took the minimum run in and, the moment he landed, applied all brakes and in a matter of a few yards came up all standing, with his nose wheel buried deeply into the very soft ground of the course.

'Some difficulty was experienced, naturally, in making communications with these people, but, after a while some of the hostages pointed out that it would be a good thing if the women and children were allowed to leave. Of course, without the engines running the air conditioning, the temperature in the plane became rather unbearable, so the nationalists agreed. A number of the people from Stanley, who had been taken on board, were allowed to leave with the passengers. Those remaining — five — were well treated. The rebels ransacked the pantry to make sandwiches for them and even offered blankets to the hostages. The nationalists themselves were feeling the cold and were huddled in blankets.

'I think that great credit must be given to the Captain of the aircraft for bringing her down safely. There could so easily have been a very nasty tragedy and, in fact, most people watching the landing, expected to see a crash. But, in fact, the plane is apparently undamaged and, apart from the wheels being sunk into the ground, is ready to go if fuel can be found and, of course, when we get the nationalists off.

'There was a certain amount of to-ing and fro-ing yesterday afternoon. The Rev. P. Millam, Senior Chaplain, and Monsignor Ireland organised a reception centre at St. Mary's for the 26 passengers who were hungry and, naturally, in some state of shock. Emissaries to the plane were allowed to collect a certain amount of baggage which was distributed as far as possible — then came the work of finding accommodation for these people. They have been housed all over the town, and appear to feel that they are being treated fairly.

'Last night Father Roel went down, by request, and held a mass on the aircraft for the nationalists in which the five hostages joined. Shortly following the mass the young lady who seems to have quite a say in the leadership, was seen to confer with her comrades and they then released the hostages.

'By this time the Defence Force had turned out in force. We never knew how strong we were — 150 past and present members were there and a guard system, with reliefs, was set out and these have been maintained. The entire area round the plane is cordoned off by the Defence Force, Marines and Police, and it was arranged for the area to be floodlit during the night. The rebels took turns, during the night, in coming out on guard.

'I should mention that when they leapt out on arrival they put up a rope and post perimeter on which were hung Argentine flags. They also handed out declarations to some people. The declarations are as usual — very badly printed — stating that the two main Islands were to be renamed Soledad and Esperanza, and Stanley to be Porto Rivero. All locally born persons would become Argentine citizens and enjoy the pleasures of that state.

'The Rev. P. Millam worked hard to get the baggage off as the women and children had nothing but what they stood up in. On his last visit to the plane they held him until about 10 *p.m.* The Captain was allowed to revisit the plane for the purpose of starting the engines to provide power for the plane' transmitters to enable the Captain and rebels to communicate with Argentina. The Captain spoke first and informed his authorities at Rio Gallegos of the position, condition of the passengers and the plane etc., after which the nationalists were allowed to speak — they assured the Argentine that they would stay with the aircraft until ordered to desist by their own people.

'You have all heard the news and their own people have quite plainly disowned them. I should think so too. Apart from the business of coming here, the very great risk they placed a number of innocent people in, including women and children, is something which can not be condoned.

'It was a quiet night, with the temperature down to 34°F and, as one the hostages has told me, they were feeling the cold when

If you want fish for supper, you can catch it!
Nancy catches an Antarctic char.

Caution, crevasse, co-metman
David Wheeler on the edge!

Good skiing locally - a rare warm sunny day.

The old PESCA whaling station at Grytviken,
now being restored and cleaned up.

Remember The Boss.
Shackleton's grave
at Grytviken.

Angry bull elephant seal – beware bad breath!

Mother and pup elephant seal.

So what's this? A gentoo penguin investigates a rain guage.

Beware ice blocks. Hestesletten ice fall.

An icy wilderness. The Hamburg and Harker glaciers.

Some glaciers enter the sea, the Lyell glacier now in retreat.

Summer snow, a blizzard can occur in summer, producing this dappling effect.

The Alps of Antarctica
Allardyce Range and Mount Paget centre from my bedroom window.

Chinese lanterns in the sky – orographic lens and pillow clouds lit up by the setting sun.

Grytviken whaling station. Two whales waiting to be flensed.

Grytviken whaling station, close up view. Stomachs cut open to release intestinal gases.

Grytviken whaling station. Whale's carcass hauled up onto flensing platform.

A giant of the ocean. A blue whale being flensed, stripped of its blubber.

Grytviken whaling station. The flenser, with knife, cuts strips of blubber off the whale.

Grytviken whaling station. Blue whale is about to be flensed. Original photo - Frank Hurley

they came off at about 8p.m. I think they must be short of food, but probably have sufficient water.

'To-day, very little has happened so far. I believe that Monsignor Ireland and the Captain went up and tried to persuade them to hand in their arms — so far without effect. On the other side — in Stanley itself we have arranged that DARWIN will sail *p.m.* on Saturday to repatriate all the passengers and possibly some of the crew, because if they can fly out, once we have gained control of the plane, they obviously will do so with minimum crew. When I heard the Captain's rather heartfelt words: "When we recover control of the plane my problem starts", I must say that I think he'll be a very brave man to try to take off, but he is convinced that he can do so. So this is the position — the passengers and some of the crew will be going on the Darwin to Montevideo.

'We hope that shortly the rebels will see the futility of their action and will lay down their arms, come out and submit to the law and order of this place.

'Amongst the passengers is the Governor of Tierra del Fuego, also a Minister of the Argentine Government for Santa Cruz, and a professional boxer who was due to fight in Rio Gallegos tonight. That is the position up to the time of this transmission.

'Since I recorded the last news there has been some development. Father Roel and the Captain of the aircraft went up there shortly after lunch and were ensconced with the rebels all the time and, I am very pleased to say, that their effort have been successful. I can not give you the exact time, but it was about 7 *p.m.* that an official announcement gave out that the whole gang had laid down their arms and were brought into Stanley under guard. The plane is in the hands of the F.I. Government and no doubt they will be thinking about how it get it away, or perhaps it will be used for a grandstand on the race-course.

'I think it was an excellent bit of work on the part of everybody concerned. A large number of people from Stanley turned out and nobody has been hurt which, surely is the way it should be.

'Goodnight.

'29/9/66

Further broadcast talk — Argentines depart 1st October

'To-day we have lost our visitors. The situation seemed slightly unclear this morning, but an Argentine transport, the BAHIA

SUSECO, appeared outside the 3-mile limit off the Lighthouse, and we had a request to keep clear of an area in Ross Road, from the Telephone Exchange to the P.W.D. Office. The prisoners were escorted down to the PHILOMEL about 10.00 this morning – my timing may not be quite right – but it was about that time that they were taken away.

'Captain White was on board giving such advice about the problems of berthing a motor fishing vessel — which is what PHILOMEL is — alongside a larger boat. In due course we heard that the swell outside — 3 miles out at sea — was too great and PHILOMEL came back again. We were again requested to keep away from that certain portion of Ross Road and the prisoners were taken back to St. Mary's Annexe. I don't know whether lunch was ready for them — it was about one o'clock.

'Later Captain White told me a little about the trip out and back. Apparently, when the prisoners boarded the PHILOMEL they started singing some rousing songs, and these continued until as far out as the Lower Tussac Island when the songs died away and there was a certain amount of unpleasantness. The prisoners had been put down in the hold and they were not all good sailors.

'When PHILOMEL reached the transport they perked up a bit, but, after some attempts to get alongside, it was decided that there was too much sea running and it was better to come back.

'I don't think very much more was heard from the prisoners until they again passed the Lower Tussac Island in Port William on the way in, when they chirped up again, or one or two did, and started singing.

'The operation of looking after the prisoners was in the charge of Sergeant Peck and other members of the Police Force, with one Marine and one member of the Defence Force, standing in the background, ready to back up the Police if circumstances warranted it. After that it was a little bit dubious about what was going to happen – the prisoners were back in St. Mary's, the passengers, who had been alerted to be ready if called for, sat round wondering what was going to happen; so did we all. This afternoon the transport was, apparently, given permission and she came into Port William where the weather was quite nice, and the prisoners were taken off again — Ross Road was again closed — and I think they had lost a certain amount of interest by this time.

'I understand that when they were loaded into the hold of the PHILOMEL they prayed for four minutes. Whether that was their trust in the navigational efforts of the crew of the PHILOMEL — which I'm sure we all know are excellent — or whether they were wondering what was going to happen to them, I have it on good authority, that they prayed for four minutes — and well they might — and then started singing again.

'This time, of course, it was a shorter trip and they sang some rousing songs all the way out, until they were alongside the Argentine vessel where the rails were lined with a considerable number, estimated to be at least 50, Argentine Marines. They were unarmed, but they were there in uniform. When the prisoners realised they were being greeted with a stony silence they tended to pipe down a bit, in fact, they shut up altogether.

'When PHILOMEL got alongside, Admiral Guzman, the Governor of the Province of Tierra del Fuego, and the captain of the aircraft went on board. They disappeared for a few minutes, and were obviously having a conference. Then the captain of the aircraft came back down the gangway and went down into the hold of the PHILOMEL. He brought up the leader, escorted him up the gangway of the transport and handed him over at the top of the ladder to what we assume are the Argentine Security Police. Then he came back and collected the young lady and took her up too — and it was noted that gentlemen went one way and the lady another on board the Argentine ship. Then up and down, up and down, up and down, until he had cleared all 19 of them.

'There was no communication at all between PHILOMEL and the Argentine ship, and the best way to sum it up is that the whole issue was carried out in stony silence.

'Then, of course, the passengers had been alerted and requested to be on the Public Jetty about 5 o'clock – but it was not until about 6 o'clock that PHILOMEL was back and took the passengers off. I understand that this transport has 20 drums of avgas on board, which PHILOMEL is going to pick up for the aeroplane, and the transport was to sail as soon as the discharge of the avgas had been completed.

'Captain White tells me that the captain of the transport had sealed orders and was unable to give any destination after the transport left here.

'The transport has left and that now leaves us with the aeroplane and four members of the crew who remained behind — the senior captain, the second pilot, the engineer and the radio officer. They are still working in the hopes of being able to get the plane out of the bog hole after which they think they can take-off.

'All seats are to be taken out of the aircraft to reduce weight. The galley and all superfluous items have already been removed. The plane is a lot further down in the ground — they managed to heave it out of the original bog hole, and then found a softer spot, where the wheels have gone further in. At the moment the plane has quite a list to starboard and the wing-tip is very, very near the ground. Anyone is able to help is assisting in every way.

'We have to think of Stanley races which are not so far off. It is going to be a big problem to fill in the holes made and made the course fit for racing.

'In was a lovely day in Stanley and most people who were able to do so visited the site to see the plane."

CHAPTER 6

A Nautical Graveyard

Wrecks around Stanley, including
the SS *Great Britain*

Soon after arriving back in Stanley, I noticed a number of shipwrecks and abandoned vessels around Stanley harbour. So during my time off meteorological duties, I decided to investigate these vessels, the most obvious of which was the *Fennia*, a four-masted Finnish barque. She had been damaged in storms near Cape Horn in 1920, brought to Stanley harbour and used as a wool storage ship by the Falkland Island Company until 1967. She was later towed to Montevideo, where she remained before being scrapped in Uruguay. I rowed out to her, but found that it was impossible to clamber aboard from my tiny rowing boat, but the wreck of the *Lady Elizabeth*, was a different matter. A pal of mine, known as 'Skip', and I rowed out to her, at the east end of the harbour, and found a large, rusty anchor chain hanging down her hull, so carefully we climbed up this — quite painful, with spiky rust flakes piercing our hands! Once on deck we had to move around very carefully; indeed, I nearly lost one more of my nine lives, when my foot plunged through a rotten bit of deck planking, revealing a 20-foot drop to the icy water sloshing about in the ship's bilges. I grabbed a nearby stanchion with one hand while Skip grabbed me, to stop me falling through the deck. That too was quite frightening!

Another interesting wreck is the *Jhelum*. She still exists at the end of a rickety walkway opposite Sullivan House. She was built in 1849, in Liverpool and traded between Europe and South America taking general cargo out, and returning to Europe with guano which is dried bird dung rich in nitrogen and copper. It is mined for its nitrates as used in fertilizers and in explosives. The *Jhelum* left Chile on July 13th 1870, was badly damaged by Cape Horn storms, and put into Stanley where the crew abandoned her, and after a survey was condemned and scuttled in her present position.

Three other vessels still in Stanley are the *Egeria*, *William Shand* and *Fleetwing*. The *Egeria* has been roofed with corrugated iron and is used as a storage space for wool and other cargoes.

The most famous shipwreck of all from the Falklands is of course I.K. Brunel's ship the *SS Great Britain*. Although I could not actually reach her in Sparrow Cove, I do recall seeing her several times from the land east of Stanley; she was very noticeable with her black and white hull. Her career, rescue and restoration make an interesting story.

By 1830, Brunel had established the Great Western Railway from London to Bristol. His next idea was to extend this service across the Atlantic, so the Great Western Steamship Service was begun using a wooden paddle steamer, the *Great Western* and Brunel decided to use a new design of ship. She was to be iron hulled and driven by a six-bladed propeller powered by an efficient steam engine producing 1000hp. She would be a sail-assisted steamship, with six masts and wire (not rope) rigging which was another innovation. Her keel was laid on 19th July 1839, in a new dry dock. She was known originally as the *Mammoth* but her name was changed to *SS Great Britain* during construction.

She was the *Queen Elizabeth* of her day, with her extraordinary size and revolutionary design. She was launched from the Great Western dock into Bristol's floating harbour, by Prince Albert on 19th July 1843. She was given a wonderful send off on July 26th 1845 on her maiden voyage to New York from Liverpool, taking 15 days at an average speed of 9.4 knots. She was a luxurious vessel for her passengers, with a stylishly decorated promenade saloon, comfy oak seats, a dining saloon with plush carpets, and ornamental pillars and a wide choice of menu.

Sadly, however, the ship was dogged by many misfortunes. In September 1846 she ran aground at Dundrum Bay in Northern Ireland, and remained there for 11 months battered and bruised by the elements, after which she was rescued and towed back to Liverpool.

Her fortunes were revived by the 19th-century Australian gold rush and she commenced a new career as an emigrant steam clipper in August 1852 and for the next 23 years carried over 15 000 passengers — that's about 50 full Jumbo jets-worth, in modern terms! During this time she was fitted with a retractable two-bladed propeller to ensure a smooth transition from steam to sail.

Her career as an emigrant ship ended in 1875, and after modifications, the removal of her engine and funnel, she was converted to a windjammer carrying cargoes of coal to America, and wheat back from America, and guano from South America to Britain. This trade brought about her demise, since, in 1886, she was badly damaged by ferocious storms off Cape Horn and she was forced to seek refuge in Port Stanley. Here she was sold to the Falkland Island Company as a storage ship which continued until 1937, when at long last she had deteriorated so badly that she had to be scuttled, and there the poor old hulk, slowing rotting, remained until in 1967, Dr Ewan Corlett, began a campaign, by writing to *The Times* newspaper to return her to Britain for restoration. So, in May 1968, the 'SS *Great Britain Project*' was launched.

A year later the millionaire business man, Jack Hayward, offered to finance this operation, and plans were made to bring her home to Bristol. In March 1970, the pontoon *Mulus III* entered Sparrow Cove, temporary repairs were made to *Great Britain*'s hull to float her and she was raised onto the pontoon to come home at last. After a 7000 mile journey from the Falkland Islands, she arrived back in Bristol to an ecstatic welcome on 5th July 1970.

She was taken to the original Great Western dock where she was built between 1839 and 1843. Here a strange event occurred. Once the dock was filled with water, tugs manoeuvred the hull into position stern first and then tractors pulled her into the dock, with clearance reduced to a few inches. Once inside with the dock gate closed, the sluice was opened to allow the dock to be drained as the tide fell. As the ship slowly settled onto the dock blocks, creaks and cracking sounds emanated from the hull, culminating in a sudden deep groan from within the hull, followed by complete silence: her old bones had found peace and comfort at last and she was at rest.

Today she has been fully restored to her former glory and in 2005, 35 years after her salvage from the Falklands she was relaunched as a major tourist attraction, after an £11.3 million restoration programme. Today visitors can go beneath a glass sea, to see the hull, walk the promenade decks, see the engine and experience how passengers lived aboard her. Brunel would have been proud of her!

Here is another interesting little story about her. On Tuesday November 16th 2010, the *Western Daily Press* carried the following article by Richard Wyatt entitled 'Nostalgia: the less famous rescue plan for *SS Great Britain*.'

This year has seen celebrations to mark the 40th anniversary of the *SS Great Britain*'s triumphant return to Bristol from a watery grave in the Falkland Islands. But I wonder how many people who visit the historic ship know of a rescue plan that was mooted 40 years before that in the 1930s. This rescue, however, was not for the benefit of the people of Bristol, but for a troop of local Sea Cadets.

The *Great Britain*'s homecoming in July 1970 was the stuff of old-fashioned adventure stories. It's reckoned 100 000 people lined the banks of the Avon to see her guided back up the river she first sailed down in December 1844. Then, in more recent years, has come a multi-million-pound conservation project vital to halting the threat of the historic ship collapsing under her own weight as her iron plates corroded. It's an intervention that has transformed Brunel's ground-breaking ship – and the dockside buildings alongside her – into a multi-award-winning museum attracting more than 170 000 people a year.

The previous rescue attempt originated in the Falklands in 1937. Devotees of the *Great Britain* – now Bristol's pride and joy – will know that, after carrying passengers to America and Australia, she was damaged in a storm off Cape Horn and made for the shelter of the Falkland Islands. Condemned as a hulk she was used to store wool and coal for 47 years before being scuttled on a sandy beach in about 15ft of water. According to a booklet produced in the Islands in 1943 to mark the centenary of the ship's launch, her owners, the Falkland Island Company, had considered offering her to the government.

On May 25, 1936 – the 50th anniversary of the ship's last voyage – it was hoped to launch an appeal for funds to secure her preservation. Letters were destined for the correspondence columns of *The Times*, a well as those of Bristol newspapers. I have searched the online archives of *The Times*, as well as council files at Bristol Record Office, for those letters but without success. Luckily for me Tansy Newman, an archivist for the Falkland Islands government, has been more successful.

She has sent me a copy of correspondence sent to the Lord Mayor of Bristol, Albert Moon, in March 1936 by the Governor of the Colony, Sir Herbert Henniker-Heaton. He apparently wanted the city to help him "save that historic ship, the Great Britain, from being towed to sea and sunk beneath these waters. Restoration will enable her to survive for many years as a memorial of the fine workmanship and material with which she was fashioned out of Bristol nearly a century ago," he continued.

Just in case the Lord Mayor was not familiar with the history of the steamship and its connections with Bristol, Sir Herbert even sent a descriptive account of the vessel's life. But this was not a fundraising exercise aimed at benefiting Bristol. Sir Herbert told the Lord Mayor that he "found it difficult to obtain ... an accurate idea of the probably cost of prolonging the life of the ship by giving her an inside cement sheath, by renewing so much of the decking as is necessary and by erecting masts and stays". In spite of this he thought that the work might cost between £5,000 and £6,000.

As well as asking *The Times* to publish a letter of appeal on May 25 he was also asking the Australian government for financial support. After all, the Great Britain had, in her long life, carried thousands of emigrants to Melbourne. Sir Herbert's plan was to make the ship the headquarters of the local Sea Rover troop.

As things turned out, the letter to *The Times* was never sent. Three weeks later the Governor sent a telegram to the Lord Mayor which read "I request no action be taken re: my letter 10th March re: restoration ship. Great Britain. Further investigations show doubtful hulk will bear strain of re-masting and cost would exceed the estimate given".

By the 1960s, however Bristol's premier daily the *Evening Post* was busy supporting the saving of a very different ship. The *Bristol Queen*, Campbell's paddle steamer had been launched from the city's Albion Dockyard in1946 and withdrawn from service in 1967. Local politician and maritime historian Sir Bob Wall was leading a campaign to try to save her from the breaker's yard.

On December 7 that year the *Evening Post* leader column noted that "the idea of a maritime symbol of Bristol's seafaring is indeed appealing — and could prove a major attraction". While moves were still afoot to bring back the *Great Britain* from the other side of the world, the *Post* thought there was a much more worthwhile preservation scheme nearer home. "That is the saving of the Bristol Queen, last of a distinguished line of Bristol Channel paddle steamers".

But fate decreed that it would be Brunel's revolutionary liner, not the *Bristol Queen*, which would become a focal point in Bristol's Harbourwide regeneration. Sir Neil Cossons, a former director of the National Maritime Museum at Greenwich, told me that the saving of the *Great Britain* was one of the finest examples of ship preservation anywhere in the world.

As curator of technology for Bristol Museum during the 1980s, Sir Neil was one of a far-sighted group of enthusiasts who decided to salvage the vessel. I often wonder if the Sea Rovers in Port Stanley ever managed to find an alternative troop hut.

CHAPTER 7

The North Atlantic Islands

Travels in Iceland, the Faroes and Spitzbergen

The North Atlantic islands of the Faroes, Iceland and Svalbard (also known as Spitzbergen) provide a dramatic contrast to Antarctica. As with Antarctica, the colder waters absorb more oxygen allowing huge fish stocks to develop, upon which seals and whales can predate. There is also of course a terrestrial top carnivore in the polar bear in the Artic which in Svalbard can be a danger to humans.

I visited the Faroe Islands in 1982, travelling on the car ferry *Smyril* from Scrabster in northern Scotland to Tórshaven, the capital of the Faroes. These islands lie halfway between Scotland and Iceland and are of volcanic origin and have a very wet climate. The main industries are farming (as family farms) and cod fishing.

The islands are not scenically very beautiful, but do possess a rather haunting atmosphere especially in the northern twilight. They are, like Iceland, a paradise for ornithologists, the bird life being abundant and diverse and it is easy to see large flocks of Golden Plover, kittiwakes and puffins, Arctic Terns and shearwaters, as well as the aggressive skuas. If you walk through the territory of either skuas or Artic Terns, you will be dive-bombed and they can hit you quite hard! Make sure you wear a hat or carry a stick.

The most endearing birds are the puffins, and of course, no one would want to eat them — or would they? Well the Faroese do eat them and a man called the Fleygamaður catches them. He has to have a good head for heights, because, to catch them, he is lowered over a cliff down to the ledges where they live. Some cliffs are up to 1000 feet high, so you don't need to be afraid of heights! Once on a ledge, he uses a net on a long pole to snare the puffins in flight, wrings their necks and ties them onto a belt around his waist, as seen in the photograph. This may seem a wasteful and cruel process to us, but it is a Faroese tradition, and relatively few puffins, from a vast population, are taken. Incidentally, puffin flesh is not fishy as you might expect, but is gamey and akin to pigeon. (I also recall eating sheep brains and whale meat, neither of which were particularly pleasant!)

Now we move north-westwards to Iceland. Its name is rather a misnomer, since the island is mainly low mountains and sand deserts and is quite green, largely due to huge areas of moss. However, Iceland also has ice sheets and glaciers.

Iceland is, however, one of the most fascinating, naturally diverse places I have ever been to and if one has an interest in biology, ornithology, geology, vulcanology, geomorphology and glaciology, then this is the place for you. Few other places on earth can pack such variety in such a small area.

My first impression of Iceland was of waking up in my tent, brightly lit with sunshine, and thinking was it time to get up. I checked my watch, only to find it was three in the morning! Being so close to the Arctic Circle, the sun hardly sets in mid summer.

I visited Iceland in 1969 and 2001, both times travelling around by overland bus. These vehicles have a high wheel base clearance, so they can ford rivers, and drive over remote areas. Revisiting a place after a long interval provides some interesting contrasts. The first contrast I experienced related to a volcanic crater called Viti, or Hell. Close to the caldera called Askja, it is a perfectly round volcanic crater, full of water. In 1969 we were warned not to descend into it, due to the danger of poisonous gases including hydrogen sulphide ('bad eggs') and sulphur dioxide (a powerful irritant) and carbon dioxide, which can asphyxiate you. In addition the water was boiling hot and not a pleasant spot for a swim. So imagine my surprise to find in 2001, that there were people swimming in it!

During the intervening years, the water had cooled to about 20°C (70°F), the gases no longer bubbled up, and it had become another thermal pool, but now with a difference — the water is yellow from suspended sulphur particles, and my wife's silver jewellery, rings and bracelets turned black, as silver sulphide formed on them! Apart from rather squishy mud, and a faint smell of sulphur, the swimming was quite pleasant.

As our bus drove around, it became clear that Icelanders have a rather different attitude to time from us. If they say the bus will arrive at 9 *a.m.*, it is 9 *a.m.* when the bus arrives, despite your watch saying something else! I like that relaxed attitude.

Camping life was pleasant. The bus would drive quite slowly to our campsites, we erected our tents, the cooks cooked and after supper there was time to explore the locality, and our guide said to be back before dark; but it does not get dark in summer!

The waterfalls are one of Iceland's glories. They include Selfoss, which you can walk behind; Skogafoss which is a beautiful, classic waterfall 60 metres high; Dettifoss, a vast, mud- and silt-laden cascade that thunders into the Hljođaklettow valley, shaking the ground as it does; Gođafoss, the 'Fall of the Gods', where Icelandic chieftains threw carvings of their gods into the water, when they rejected paganism, and adopted Christianity; and finally Gullfoss, the 'Golden Falls', near Geysir. Here the water cascades over two ledges at different angles to each other. Gullfoss is probably the best-known waterfall, being on the tourist trail out from Reykjavick.

Iceland is rightly known as the land of ice and fire. Water and fire are wonderful servants, but cruel masters, and when the two combine, as when an eruption happens beneath an ice cap, devastation occurs. This happened with the great eruptions of the seventeenth and eighteenth centuries, and as recently as the Grimsvötn eruption beneath the Vatnajökull in 1996 and of course the Eyjafjallajökull eruption in 2010. If a sub-ice eruption occurs, vast floods of melt water, ice blocks, silt and mud burst out of the glacier and cause devastating floods. These outburst floods are called 'hlaups', so an eruption of the Katla volcano in 1823 caused a 'katlahlaup' — a Katla flood.

So, why is Iceland volcanic? Iceland straddles the Mid-Atlantic Ridge where the African and American tectonic plates are being pulled apart at about two cms (about an inch) a year. This creates the Mid-Atlantic Ridge which is a line of weakness in the earth's crust, allowing magma to rise through it, creating volcanoes and causing earthquakes. Where the Mid-Atlantic Ridge passes through Iceland, it is marked by a belt of volcanoes, hot springs, steam springs (geysers) and solfataras, and other places of high volcanic activity, about 40 miles wide.

One of these areas is near to Lake Mŷvatn (Midge Lake), and it is an amazing place of hot bubbling mud pools. Don't fall in — you will be boiled alive! Here also you will find steaming sinter cones as steam is forced out of the ground under pressure, together with highly coloured deposits of sulphur. It was also here in 1969 that we swam in an underground rock pool, inside a crack in the lava; impossible now as the temperature had soared to almost boiling point.

Icelanders are a great people for making use of anything that nature offers them, so here we found a sauna hut, directly over a steaming hot fumarole, with hot gas and steam issuing between the legs of squatting Icelanders — a bit smelly to say the least. Rather like a hot fart, in reverse!

A great deal of work is being done here with thermal plants to tap this geothermal energy and many Icelandic homes are now heated in this way. Landmannalaugar is another geothermal centre, where warm water flows out from below a lava field and has been channelled into rock pools in which people can swim, and I recall swimming at midnight, drinking curaçao in the lovely warm water!

Ice is the other spectacular geological force that shapes inland Iceland. There are four main ice caps, all remnants from the last Ice Age, the largest being the Vatnajökull in south-east Iceland, which covers about one sixth of the island. The glaciers emerging from Vatnajökull used to reach the sea, but they have retreated and at Jökulsárlón have left a spectacular iceberg-covered lake. The Icelanders, always quick to cash in on nature's beauty, have created a visitor centre from which boats, seemingly converted DUKWs, or landing craft, drive around among the icebergs, giving dramatic views of the ice caps, icebergs and the intensely blue water and sky — magnificent! On the visit, it was at this point that the boat stopped nearby an iceberg so that we could hack off chunks of 1000 year-old ice for our G&Ts.

Vatnajökull is curious because it is a temperate ice cap, i.e. it could not grow from scratch under today's conditions, but because it is already there, it creates and maintains its own local climate which sustains it. Moreover, it is close to melting point, at any given depth in its profile, except in the top layers which remain frozen all year round.

Icelandic wildlife is prolific and in the case of bird life is highly visible and quite approachable. We saw large flocks of puffins, Golden Plovers and Arctic Terns and petrels. However, as already noted, the skuas and Arctic Terns must be treated with caution!

At the top of the food chain, Gyr Falcons and Snowy Owls occur, both of which we were privileged to see, causing the 'twitchers' in the group a lot of excitement. Another example of cashing in on nature's bounty nowadays is to provide whale-watching trips, so the whale-catching boats now carry tourists instead of harpoon gunners, although some whaling still occurs. One hopes they can make more money out of showing the whales to tourists rather than killing them.

We boarded a whaler at Húsavík and trundled around Skjálfandi Bay for about two-and-a-half hours. If you saw a whale, which we did, you had to shout a clock time number, relative to the bow(which was 12 o'clock) so a whale just off the starboard bow was 'whale one o'clock'. Several pilot whales and a humpback whale were seen blowing and 'fluking', that is raising their tails in the air as they dive.

Finally, a word about Icelandic food. Today most towns possess supermarkets and you have the varieties of foods available at home, but this was not always the case. Up to the Second World War, when Iceland was occupied by the Allies, the diet was limited to what could be grown in the difficult climate, or caught either in the sea or air.

I have already mentioned the Fleygamaður of the Faroes, and Icelanders eat puffins as well, but we sampled other curious delicacies, laid on for us in a lava cave! The starter was rotted shark, tasting quite ammoniacal, and was washed down with brennivin which is local vodka. This was followed by dried and boiled fish with buttery blood pudding and singed sheep's head, then ram's testicles and potatoes! The pudding was rice pudding with raisins and cinnamon! Follow that as they say; but again, it reflects the Icelanders' reliance on local products in the past. I have no doubt that today most of them prefer food from the supermarkets however.

The Icelanders are delightful people, very cultured, very independently minded, and very proud of their little country which stands on the very edge of the Arctic and which nowadays is self-sufficient in electrical and geothermal energy, and is a magnet for tourists.

And, so, to the northern 'edge of the world' — the archipelago of Svalbard. This group of islands is more commonly known to British people as Spitzbergen, but Spitzbergen is only the largest and only inhabited island, its name meaning 'pointed rock'. I visited these islands in July 1996, sailing from Tromsø in northern Norway on board the MS Nordstjernen, 'North Star'. This was a tough, ice-strengthened ship, built in 1956 for the Hurtigruten or coastal voyage routes. She was rather similar to the *RRS John Biscoe*, but a lot more comfortable, and, with only about 90 passengers aboard, was a delight to sail on. I believe she is still sailing the Hurtigren routes in 2010 which indicates her reliability and quality of building.

Two days out of Tromsø we approached the islands through fog and drizzle and a temperature of around 3°C (37°F) which gave a rather eerie atmosphere to the place. These islands lie about 200 miles north of northern Norway, between North Cape and the North Pole. They are fairly mountainous but heavily glaciated. They became a centre of whaling in the seventeenth century and were a departure point for polar expeditions, including Amundsen's venture with the air ship *Norge*, and Nobile's with the airship *Italia*. The capital, Longyearbyen, is named after the manager of the Arctic Coal Company, John Munroe Longyear. Coal is still mined on the islands as we shall see later on.

Our first port of call was Longyearbyen, where you truly get the feeling of a frontier town: men dressed in thick furs, even in summer, carrying rifles for protection against polar bear attacks; large piles of wood stored by the houses; skis; snow mobiles; and tents for hire or sale. Polar bears are of course protected, but you can shoot them in self-defence, but only as a last resort. Most people use trip wires, flares and even bird scarers to drive them away, but they are fast, powerful, aggressive and very inquisitive creatures, so can be very dangerous. Indeed, two tourists were attacked and eaten in their camp, the year I visited, so always beware.

After Longyearbyen, we sailed north to Magdalene Fiord, where we disembarked and went ashore. This is a former whaling centre but with no factories here. Instead whales were caught, dragged ashore, dismembered on the spot and the blubber rendered down to oil. Bones lie scattered all around you, and even today there's a feeling of death about this place. Two crew members, armed with rifles, kept a lookout for polar bears. Sadly, none were seen that day, but I do not think that they would have been shot!

We then sailed out of Magdalene Fiord, and turned north-east through the narrow and dramatic Smeerenburg Fiord, its steep glaciated and rocky sides creating a dark and threatening atmosphere — even today being shipwrecked here would be life threatening. Then we were through the rocky channels and out into

The Fleygamadur – puffin catcher. Puffin meat is not fishy, but is gamey, like pigeon.

Puffins, birds found in their thousands on Faroese cliffs.

High cliffs and rough seas are typical of the Faroe Islands.

Icebergs at Jokulsarlon. The Vatnajökull has retreated leaving a lake full of icebergs 1000 years old.

Glacier flowing down from Eyjafjallajokull. Remember the eruption of April 2010.

Eruption of Grimsvotn volcano under the Vatnajökull caused massive outburst floods in 1996.

Night time eruption, Askja volcano, 1963

Columnar jointing of basalt lava flow

Snow, ice, water and steam, climbing near Landmannalaugar

Godafoss

Skogafoss

Dettifoss

Waterfalls abound in Iceland

*Use of geothermal heat –
tropical greenhouse, garden of Eden!*

*Use of geothermal heat – bathing in hot
pools at Landmannalaugar, Iceland.*

Glacier flowing from ice-cap into Billefjorden, Svalbard

The Waggon Way Glacier, Spitzbergen

Sea ice off Svalbard

Red rock, white ice, blue sea. A 'bergy bit' off Spitzbergen in midnight sunshine.

Polar bears on ice floes

Purple saxifrage, Svalbard

Roald Amundsen, Arctic hero and explorer

Ny-Alesund town band, scientists working at the research centre welcome visitors.

the Arctic Ocean with 400 miles to the North Pole, heading to Moffen Island.

As we approached the Island, the cry went up 'ice ahead' and there it was, the southern edge of the Arctic ice cap. It was such a dramatic moment when you realise how far north you really are at 80° North 14° East. At this moment, we were perhaps the most northerly people in the world — 'on top of the world'" at the farthest north you could get by commercial vessel at that time. Since then however, the Russians have begun North Pole cruises using nuclear-powered ice- breakers — rather unfair I feel!

Moffen Island is the home of many walruses, powerful, tusked, seal-like creatures who dominate the ecosystem here, but can be attacked by the top predator, the polar bear.

The ship then turned south into Wood Fiord, and as we did so the sun came out. This of course is the midnight sun; low, bright and with a reddish tinge, it illuminated the mountains in the background beautifully as seen in the photos which were taken at 11.30 *p.m.*

Ny-Ålesund on Kongsfjorden was our next stop, and we were welcomed by the town's seven-piece band, a bizarre sight and sound here in the Arctic wilderness. This is an ex-coal-mining town and to this day there is a small steam engine and five trucks perched on sections of rail track; 'the train to nowhere'! Ny-Ålesund's main claim to fame is that it was the departure point for many polar explorers, and expeditions. The town centre is dominated by a massive bust of Roald Amundsen, the explorer who beat Captain Scott to the South Pole. Amundsen explored the Arctic between 1905 and 1928, but took a break in 1912 to conquer the South Pole; such was the determination and experience of this amazing man.

In 1905 Amundsen and his crew set sail in *Gjoa*, from Norway to find the North-west Passage. Having become trapped in ice, they continued by dog-sled arriving at a place called Eagle Alaska, 540 miles away, thus being the first men to traverse the North-west Passage. In 1909, Amundsen was preparing to travel to the North Pole, but he heard that Robert Peary had arrived there first. So, he immediately switched his attention to the South Pole, organised an expedition, overtook Captain Scott's expedition, and arrived there on December 14th 1911.

Amundsen then decided to explore the Arctic again and so, on

May11th 1926, he set out to fly from Svalbard to Alaska. The aircraft crashed short of the Pole, and he and his crew were rescued. However, being such a determined man, he tried again next year, with the American Lincoln Ellsworth, and the Italian explorer Umberto Nobile. He crossed the Pole 16 hours after leaving Ny-Ålesund, and, three days later, having flown 3274 miles, they landed triumphantly in Alaska, thus being the first men to have flown across the top of the world. Amundsen and his fellow explorers were indeed heroic figures.

Sadly in May 1928, tragedy struck: Umberto Nobile's new airship *Italia*, launched from Ny-Ålesund, crashed in the Arctic Ocean onto the ice. Amundsen organised a rescue effort, with five other men, and set off by air to look for him, but three hours later Amundsen's plane crashed and nobody knew where. Thus perished a magnificent explorer in the act of trying to rescue another explorer — a truly great man. Ironically, Nobile and his crew were rescued a few days later. So, you will see, dear reader, why Ny-Ålesund is a place of such great historic importance, in the history of Arctic exploration. Ny-Ålesund is now an international research base, researching atmospherics, climatology and glaciology.

Another aspect of Svalbard is its coal mining industry. Early explorers and trappers discovered coal and it began to be mined in 1906, by the Arctic Coal Company run by John Longyear. This company was taken over by Store Norsk Spitsbegen Kulcompani A/S (SNSK) which has run the coal mines ever since. Coal is mined in Longyearbyen, and in the Russian settlement of Barentsburg.

A visit to Barentsburg takes you back to an atmosphere of the old Soviet Union in the days of the Cold War. Although the Russians in Barentsburg were very friendly, the grimy buildings, the black smoke from the central- heating system, and the political slogans, exhorting hard work and love for the Motherland , all contributed to this curious and outdated atmosphere. The mining town is struggling to survive, money is short, it is in a state of disrepair, but they put on a display of folk dancing and music which was cheerful and jolly. But as soon as they were finished, it was back to the stalls selling trinkets, USSR military medals and samovars!

The Russian's presence in Svalbard is purely political, because under the Svalbard Treaty signed in 1920, they have equal mining rights on the islands, although Norway has sovereignty over them. Coal mining today is not really economic but, by maintaining the industry there, Russia keeps a foothold in the islands.

Although Svalbard is a long way off the beaten track, for anyone with an interest in the Arctic, it is a fascinating place to visit, and I feel very privileged to have been there.

CHAPTER 8

Return to Antarctica

A journey by sea from Tierra del Fuego to Antarctica
and back via the Falklands and South Georgia

When I started work for the then Ministry of Agriculture, now DEFRA, after my return from the Falklands in 1966, my then boss, Mr David Inns, asked me one day, if I had a life assurance policy. At the time I did not, so he gave me the Sun Life of Canada rep's card and I proceeded to set up a policy, paying what nowadays would seem the ridiculously small sum of £9.00 per month.

Over the years, the sum and the benefits accumulated, and in 1999 a rep told me that, when I reached 60 in 2003, it would be worth around £40,000! You can imagine my astonishment.

However, this was not to be, because other events intervened; in September 2011, terrorists attacked the World Trade Centre twin towers in New York and the world's economy took a dive. The final value of the life assurance policy fell to £28,000 but this was still enough to finance a return journey to Antarctica for myself and a first time visit for my wife, Barbara.

So we contacted Peregrine Expeditions, who run expedition cruises to the Falkland Islands and the Antarctic Peninsula, and booked ourselves on an 18-night cruise which would take us from Ushuaia, in southern Argentina, to the Falklands, South Georgia, and the Antarctic Peninsula, weather conditions permitting. However, before this journey we decided to have a look at Argentina, so we added on five days in Buenos Aires, and three days in Ushuaia.

Late January 2004, in London was cold and sleety, but on arrival in Buenos Aires, the 30°C heat hit us! Our hotel provided an excellent English-speaking contact called Christina who proved very helpful.

After check in at the hotel, we needed to eat, and after walking around locally, discovered a nearby restaurant. Beef is the premier food in Argentina, and whatever one thinks of the meat, this beef was delicious — beautifully flavoured, slightly fatty and so tender — the best we had ever eaten! One amusing incident occurred here. The sign for the peso is $ as it is for US dollars, which were also usable. There were about 30 pesos to the dollar — we paid in dollars, no wonder the waiter looked pleased!

A city orientation tour gave us our bearings, but it was walking about that showed us the extremes in this city. While the very rich (and there are plenty of them) can afford dog walkers who groom, feed, and walk groups of dogs around the city by day, the poor immigrants move in from the suburbs to scavenge for food, recyclables and used goods from dumps and skips, while feral dogs scavenge around them.

Our next excursion, was very touristy, but it gave us a good insight into one aspect of Argentine culture, that of the gaucho, the tough Indian of the Pampas, who now is the Argentine equivalent of the American cowboy. These guys are skilled horsemen, driving herds of cattle across the Pampas in heat and dust, living rough and earning a pittance, but they love the life. At Estancia Susannah, we were treated to displays of cattle round-ups, rodeo riding, and lassoing using the *boleadoras*, an especially Argentinean way of catching cattle. The gaucho spins a rope, to which three leather balls are attached and lets them fly at the intended target beast. The balls spin as they fly and they are intended to wrap themselves around the animal's horns. The gaucho then tightens the rope to haul the beast in. This, however, is all done from the saddle while riding at speed — an amazing skill! Don't try it at home.

The *South American Handbook*, an invaluable guide, recommended a trip to the World Heritage Site of Colonia del Sacramento in Uruguay. So, we set out on a fast ferry, the *Buquebus*, from Buenos Aires, across the vast River Plate which is wider than the English Channel at this point.

Colonia is fascinating, a throwback to Spanish colonial times, a sleepy, old-fashioned place, with beautiful tree-lined avenues, lovely shady squares and a charming and drowsy atmosphere. It was quiet, peaceful, and hot and while we ate, parakeets and bee-eaters darted about in the trees. Cobbled streets led down to the water front, where spectacular sunsets, caused by the atmospheric pollution from Buenos Aires, can be seen. We found several museums, one of armadillos, one of fans and another of tiles — an eclectic mixture. Take your pick!

Argentina is 1200 miles long, and it takes over two hours to fly from Buenos Aires to Ushuaia, but it was an interesting flight, because in the far west, one could see the snowy outline of the Andes, the world's longest mountain range.

We had three days in Ushuaia; have you ever been to a 'gold rush' town? This was one, only the 'gold' comes not out of the ground, but out of tourists' pockets, as about 30 cruise ships call there each summer on their way to Antarctica or around the world.

Ushuaia was built largely by convicts in the nineteenth century using wood from local forests, so a narrow-gauge railway was built for transport. Penal colonies were used to populate Tierra del Fuego. A replica train exists today, known as *el Tren del Fin del Mundo*, which now ferries tourists back and forth, and is driven by English engine drivers, who go there for the season!

Another fascinating aspect of Ushuaia is the pre-European Indian culture of the Ona, Yamana and Selk'nam, aboriginal peoples. Sadly they were almost eradicated by cattle ranchers and diseases, notably measles, but came to the notice of the British public when Capt Robert FitzRoy brought four of them back to Britain, and they were given the extraordinary names of Jeremy (or Jemmy) Button, York Minster, Fuegia Basket and Boat Memory. They became quite famous and were shown off around the country, even at one point meeting King William IV.

So after a brief but fascinating look at this remote part of Argentina, we embarked on our ship, the *Akademic Ioffe*, to sail to the Falkland Islands and Antarctica. She was built in 1989 in Rauma, Finland, as a scientific research vessel for the Russian Academy of Science, Institute of Oceanology. She was named after the academic Abraham Ioffe, a nuclear physicist with the Russian Academy of Sciences, who proceeded to lead a research institute in St. Petersburg.

She was ordered by the Soviet Navy basically to listen to and record acoustic signatures of American submarines below the Arctic ice. However, with the fall of communism, the Russian Navy could no longer afford her, so she was modified to take passengers to polar regions on expedition cruises, and being ice-strengthened, was an ideal vessel.

She was fairly basic, the food was filling and good. Facilities included a bar, library, public lounge and dining hall, and the ship had an 'open bridge' policy. So shipboard life was comfortable, but not luxurious.

The first leg of our return to Antarctica took us to the Falkland Islands, and a landing at Devil's Nose Bay, on West Point Island, where Rockhopper Penguins and Albatrosses live while skuas and caracaras prey on penguin chicks, demonstrating that nature is truly red in tooth and claw, as food chains operate so clearly here.

After watching the skuas feed, we needed our own sustenance, which came in the form of a famous Falklands Tea, provided by the Napier family in their farmhouse. These teas are now quite well known, but how they provide them for 1000 or more passengers from large cruise ships is amazing. The answer is a full-time Chilean chef, several helpers and a dedicated bakery behind the house!

The next day we arrived at Stanley, which was quite an emotional return for me, after 38 years, and I was fascinated to see how Stanley had changed. I wanted to see my old lodgings at 5, Crozier Place, now the HQ of an environmental cleaning firm. I was welcomed in by an office worker who told me that they have several ex-BAS staff calling in annually to view the house. Such changes; no peat-fired range to bake that wonderful bread Dorothy Biggs produced, no chooks for those blood-red eggs, and all our rooms now offices! When looking out over the harbour here, I had an extraordinary feeling ,a flashback to my time there — very weird.

So, how much had Stanley changed? Many of the warehouses along the seafront had become souvenir shops, full of Chinese-made plastic penguins! A new supermarket had appeared, internet connections are available, the Globe Inn had become a South Atlantic Bistro-bar and the HQ of the occupying Argentine forces had become a war museum.

I also noticed that central heating had replaced peat. Few people kept chickens and fewer sheep were kept, so the population had become far less self-sufficient, but set against these changes much more income was made for the Islands, from fishing licences, and of course tourism and consequently there was a general atmosphere of prosperity and well-being. This was quite different from my first visit, when one had the feeling that the Islands really were a bit of a colonial backwater, of little interest to Britain.

And so, after Stanley, we set sail once again, east-by-south, towards South Georgia. This leg was remarkable for its tranquillity with a slight swell, some mist, and low cloud intermittently broken by glimpses of the sun. So imagine our surprise and delight when, on the 9th of February, we awoke to bright sunshine, blue sky, and the glaciated mountain peaks of the coast of South Georgia looming ahead.

A couple of Zodiac cruises to the shore and around the Welcome Islands now revealed the wealth of wildlife here. It included albatrosses, Cape Petrels, Sheath Bills, King Macaroni and Rockhopper Penguins, the South Georgia Pipit (causing great excitement among the twitchers), not forgetting fur and elephant seals. Nothing however had prepared us for our next stop: 'Penguin City', otherwise known as Salisbury Plain. We all see the wonders of wildlife on our TV screens; and this place indeed is a wildlife wonder, up there with polar bears, elephants, vast shoals of fish, or even the Great Barrier Reef! Fifty thousand breeding pairs of King Penguins live here. Can a camera bring you the noise (shrieks, squeals, gurgles, barks and clackings), the smell (a cross between rotting fish and dirty nappies), the mud (glutinous or fluidic, mixed with penguin shit — just like fishy diarrhoea? No it can not!

Once you have got used to these little inconveniences and you settle down to watch them, you realise that they are fascinating birds, exhibiting, in a relatively small area, every possible apparently human characteristic — loving tenderness, squabbling, preening, displaying, nipping, clouting with wings, and general gossip and chatting. I sat among the tussock grass, quite close to a group for about an hour, absolutely entranced by them — truly a wildlife wonder of the world. However, perhaps I have anthropomorphised them too much.

You see many immature birds covered in a fluffy brown down, which led many early explorers to believe that they were a different species, the 'Downy Penguin'. My wife observed an amusing incident here, involving these immature birds. Two adults were 'chatting' by a vigorous clacking of beaks vertically upwards, when a downy penguin approached asking for food. Whack went a wing, and the poor creature had to push off. No food there then!

Onward towards Grytviken, but en route a small diversion. The ship anchored in Fortuna Bay so that several of us could disembark and walk from the Bay over to Stromness, a former whaling station. This is the Shackleton Way, commemorating the easiest and last stretch of Sir Ernest Shackleton's trek, which he undertook with three men and 30 feet of rope from Pegotty Camp, after his journey from Elephant Island. Most people will have heard of Shackleton's epic journey by small boat, the *James Caird*, from Elephant Island to South Georgia in 1915, described in the book *The Worst Journey in the World*.

And so we proceeded to Grytviken, the 'capital' of South Georgia. By tradition nowadays the first stop is Shackleton's grave, to drink a toast to the 'Boss'. You raise your glass, drink almost all the beer, then pour the remainder onto the grave, so the worms must be well pickled by now!

It was wonderful to return here. Superficially little had changed and so my picture of Mount Hodges towering over Grytviken Harbour was still accurate, but the whaling station is being cleaned up, the little church has been restored and dedicated as a memorial church to Sir Ernest Shackleton, and the manager's house has become an excellent if rather gruesome museum of whaling. Shackleton House, my home on King Edward Point, has been replaced by more up-to-date and environmentally friendly accommodation and laboratories.

As we sailed out of King Edward Cove into Cumberland East Bay, the magnificent panorama of the Allardyce Range came into view, and for me this was a nostalgic, rather bitter–sweet moment, not only reminding me of the view from my accommodation in Shackleton House in 1966, but also that it would probably be the last time I would see it!

After departing Grytviken in the evening, we sailed south-east towards Gold Harbour, intending to land. However the weather deteriorated rapidly and a full gale blew up, so Zodiac landings were cancelled and we hove to in the lee of an enormous, tabular iceberg half a mile long. It was certainly the biggest I have ever seen, but still small by comparison with some tabular bergs as they break off ice shelves. They are large, flat pieces of ice shelf that break off from huge ice sheets such as the Ross Ice Shelf in Antarctica. They break off for a number of reasons including the effects of cracking, drag from ocean currents and the wind, or their colossal mass being too much to be supported at the edge of a floating ice shelf. Tabular bergs are flat topped, looking rather like colossal aircraft carriers. Indeed there were plans in World War Two to tow some from

Antarctica, coat them with a special type of concrete surface layer, and use them as such! Given that this one was about 200 feet high and that nine-tenths of the ice is below the surface it must have been about 2000 thick! Amazing to see such an object.

We landed on Elephant Island on St Valentine's Day 2004 in difficult conditions, high winds and rough seas, which gave us just a taste of the conditions that Shackleton and his tiny crew and boat had to endure. Shackleton was an inspiring leader who put his men's safety above his own glory, and consequently never lost a man.

Later that day the ship passed a rocky outcrop called Brown Bluff, at the head of the Antarctic Sound, and for me a great moment; Antarctica at last! The next day we landed on Joinville Island which as you can see in the photograph is a haven for wildlife, with fur seals, elephant seals and Adelie Penguins. Here again we saw the natural operation of the food chain in action when skuas attacked a penguin chick and dragged it away from its parents to dismember it. However this provoked an outcry amongst some of our fellow passengers. But, as I pointed out to them, you really cannot interfere in natural process. The skuas have young to feed as well. This visit was memorable for the colourful and varied shapes of icebergs, as shown in the photographs.

One of the eeriest places that we visited was Deception Island, which lies between King George Island and the Antarctic Peninsula. There is an abandoned British Antarctic Survey base there, dilapidated buildings, with wind whistling through them, corrugated iron sheets flapping, an abandoned Auster plane, and Chinstrap Penguins wandering about, combining to give it a spooky atmosphere.

In February 1944, a British base (Base B) was set up here by the Royal Navy. This was called 'Operation Tabarin' and it terminated in 1945 when the buildings were given to the Falkland Islands Dependencies Survey (FIDS). This was the forerunner of the British Antarctic Survey. The base has had a chequered history. In 1946 the main accommodation hut burnt down, and in 1967 and 1969, volcanic eruptions occurred, the latter one causing its closure. The base has been tidied up now and remains as an historic site, as monument number 71 under the Antarctic Treaty.

Sailing on southwards past the Palmer Coast, we came next day to Cuverville Island. The whole place was under fresh snow which provided great sport for the local Gentoo Penguins, which, like us, enjoy tobogganing. They would waddle about a 100 metres up a slope then slide down on their bellies head first ,a bit like the louche in the winter Olympics!

Later that day we were out in the Zodiacs again to observe whales in Wilhemena Bay. Drive out, cut the motor and wait ... soon they will come near to investigate the boat. 'Not too near,' I thought, as one flip of their flukes and we'd be swimming in the icy water, or perhaps imitating Jonah! A word of warning to prospective whale watchers however: don't get within 50 metres downwind of their breath which is an appalling stench, a cross between rotting fish and bad eggs — and put that cigarette out!

And so, on to our final day in Antarctica, which brought us to Paradise Bay and Neko Harbour. These two places provided a fitting climax to our cruise along the Palmer Coast, being the most spectacular settings around them both that we had ever seen. On arrival we set out from the ship across to the now closed Argentine base of Almirante Brown and from there climbed up a steep snow slope to a point over looking this bay. Below us was a tiny beach and a rocky promontory set against a backdrop of massive glaciers, sweeping steeply down into the bay, cracking and booming as they calved their icebergs. Some of these were eroded into fantastic shapes, like the one shown, which reminded me of the Monument to the Discoveries outside Lisbon in Portugal. From our eyrie atop this cliff top viewpoint, we turned our life jackets into toboggans, and slid down back to the base — quite exhilarating!

After this we set out in the Zodiacs, which proved to be a mini wildlife cruise. Our Zodiac was circled by a most inquisitive Gentoo Penguin, which twice dived under the Zodiac — looking for titbits perhaps — then we were dive-bombed by a most aggressive skua which repeatedly tried to scalp me! I don't think it would have enjoyed eating my scalp though; a bit tough probably.

At this point, 65°S 64°W, we had reached the most southerly point of our voyage. Indeed winter was beginning to make its first appearance by the freezing over of the water in Paradise Harbour, as illustrated by the appearance of pancake ice. And so, reluctantly, our ship turned its bows to the north-west into the straits between Anvers and Brabante Islands, and ultimately towards Cape Horn. As we prepared to leave Paradise Harbour, there was a sudden commotion in the water, and two humpback whales dived beneath the ship then reappeared on the port side briefly before diving again and fluking. It was as if they were saying farewell to us!

As we passed through the straits, we saw our sister ship the *Academik Sergei Vavilov* with whom we exchanged lively greetings!

The last goodbye however occurred later in the evening, after supper, when we decided to take a breath of fresh air, and indeed to get a last glimpse of Antarctica. Luck was with us, for there on our starboard beam were the mountains of the Palmer Coast, backlit by the rays of the setting sun, the delicate shades of pink and orange leaving a beautiful farewell picture in our minds as a fitting end to our journey.

We had of course only touched the fringes of Antarctica, but the sheer immensity of the ice caps, glaciers and mountains, together with the tastes of wild weather, had given us lasting impressions of this most magnificent, remote and yet potentially fragile and beautiful continent.

CHAPTER 9

The Foreseeable Future of the Polar Regions

In this chapter I will try to explain the background to two concerns about the polar regions. The first is a relatively local concern, while the other is global.

The first concern is the ongoing dispute between Britain and Argentina over the Falkland Islands. So, what is the history of these islands, and why is there a dispute? These islands lie between 51° and 53° south and 57° and 62° west, in the south Atlantic, about 300 miles due east of Argentina. It is now thought that they are not part of South American geology.

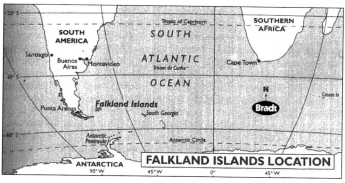

When the supercontinent of Gondwanaland broke up, the Falklands were thought to have been attached to the large piece which became southern Africa. As this moved east through tectonic plate movements, the Falklands became separated and remained near South America. This is indicated by geological similarities to rocks in southern Africa.

The first British claim to the discovery of the Islands was a sighting by Captain John Davis, of the *Desire* on August 14th

1592. William Dampier reached the islands in 1684, and Captain John Strong of the Sloop *Welfare* landed at Port Howard on West Falkland in 1690 and he named the straight between the East and West Falklands as Falkland Sound in honour of Viscount Falkland, Treasurer of the English Navy.

In 1740, Lord Anson arrived and he planned to use the Islands as a base for exploring the Pacific Ocean. However, the Spanish objected to this, saying it would cause instability, since they claimed the region under the Treaty of Tordesillas, signed between Spain and Portugal in 1494. In 1493, Pope Alexander IV, in a Papal bull or proclamation, had decided that henceforth all territories discovered to the west of a line north to south, 100 leagues west of the Azores, or discovered south of the Azores or Cape Verde Islands, should belong to Spain. The fact that Portugal was not mentioned in the bull prompted negotiations between Portugal and Spain resulting in the Treaty of Tordesillas which agreed that all lands to the west of a line 370 Castilian leagues (approximately 1281 miles) west of the Cape Verde Islands would become Spanish (excepting Brazil, which was already Portuguese) and those to the east of the line would become Portuguese.

England, however, did not agree with this decision and sent further expeditions by Drake, Raleigh and Cavendish. In April 1764, Louis de Bougainville arrived in East Falkland from St Malo, in France, to establish Port Louis and naming the Islands 'Isles Malouines' derived from St Malo, and converted to 'Islas Malvinas' by the Argentines. We must remember that at this time Argentina did not exist as an independent nation, but Spain was occupying East Falkland from 1770 until 1811, and lost its empire during this period. Argentina became independent from Spain in 1816 and in 1820 sent Colonel David Jewett, a privateer from the United States in the employ of a Buenos Aires businessman, to assert ownership rights of the Islands in place of Spain, this being while the Islands were de facto ungoverned, although claimed by Britain.

After various skirmishes and minor attempts at re-occupation, Captain Onslow arrived in 1833 to reassert British sovereignty and removed the then Argentinian occupiers by force. In 1840, the British Government allowed and encouraged settlers from Britain to go to the Islands to start ranching and other businesses. It must be pointed out that there were no native or indigenous people living in these islands, at this time, or any other, as far as can be ascertained. In 1845 a new town was completed in East Falkland, called Port Stanley, now the capital.

So to summarise the position: Argentina claimed the islands under the Papal bull of the fifteenth century, while Britain claimed them for two reasons: firstly, claiming the first recorded landing in 1690 and, secondly, having been in open and continuously effective occupation since 1833, a position accepted by the United Nations in 1982. So possession being 'nine tenths of the law', the islands became British. Although a colony, the occupation of the islands by Britain did not involve removing, killing, or subjugating an indigenous population, which did occur in Argentina as Patagonia was developed for ranching.

The present residents of the Islands are of mainly British descent and to hand them over to Argentina would create an Argentine colony, completely at odds with the United Nation's position on decolonisation. This in essence states that the majority of residents in a referendum should state a wish to secede from a colonial ruler before independence can take place.

Relations with Argentina deteriorated between 1964 and 1976, when the *RRS Shackleton* was fired on by an Argentine gunboat and an illegal military base was set up on Southern Thule, an island near South Georgia, but despite these incidents trade and air connections with Argentina grew, and had not General Galtieri jumped the gun in 1982, I believe that an amicable arrangement on sovereignty could have been reached. However, as we are all aware, no such agreement was reached, and the rest, as they say, is history.

As a result of the conflict, so ably won by the Royal Navy and the British Army under extremely difficult conditions and at a vast distance, the Islands were recovered and Argentina was subsequently liberated from a dreadful fascist government. However, Argentina does continue to claim the Islands, but nowadays by peaceful means only.

Recent developments concerning oilfield exploration and development must not be deflected by political posturing by the Argentine government, who regularly use the 'Malvinas Question' to raise support for themselves, among the voters. My own impression, when Argentineans raised the subject of the Malvinas, was that they did not really care about the Islands and certainly would not want to live there!

So, are there any possible grounds for some kind of agreement over the Falkland Islands? Possibly so, as long as Argentina accepts that the wishes of the Islanders are paramount, as accepted by the United Nations. In March 2009, Prime Minister Gordon Brown stated in a meeting with the Argentinian President that there would be no talks over the future of the Falklands.

However, if oil in commercial quantities, is found, arrangements could be made for Argentina, as well as Britain and the Falklands, to benefit. This could involve arrangements for Argentina to provide infrastructure in the form of rig construction and maintenance, supplies of materials and labour, all of which would bring major benefits to Argentina. Such arrangements exist between Britain and Norway today, to the mutual benefit of both nations.

Sovereignty of the Islands, however, is not up for discussion since the vast majority of the Islanders wish to remain as a dependent territory of the UK and any attempt to alter that position would be seen as an unacceptable betrayal not only of the Islanders living there today, but also of all the brave service men and women who gave their lives to liberate the Islands from foreign rule in 1982.

The second area of concern about the polar regions is the effect of global warming and climate change. The principal questions are these: are human activities causing the temperature of the atmosphere to rise, and what might be the effects on the planet and humanity generally, as well as specifically on the polar regions?

Let's look at some basic facts:

1. Our atmosphere acts as an insulating — i.e., heat retaining — blanket, just like a duvet, keeping the planet warm with an average temperature of around 14.5 °C. If it was absent, apart from the fact that we could not breathe, we and all life would quickly freeze to death, so some heat retention is vital. This is the 'Greenhouse effect'.

2. Certain gases, notably carbon dioxide (CO_2), methane (CH_4) and water vapour are better at retaining heat than others, so, in principle, the more of these gases there are in our atmosphere, the greater the temperature rise. This is known as the *Enhanced Greenhouse effect*.

How does this work? Solar heat passes through the atmosphere and heats the earth's surface. This heat, as infra-red radiation, is reflected back towards space but is trapped by the increased concentration of greenhouse gases, thus warming the atmosphere around the world.

5 Crozier Place, former lodgings in Stanley.

Whalebone arch, Stanley

Gentoo penguin colony, Carcass Island

King penguins on Salisbury Plain, South Georgia.

King penguins and fur seals, Salisbury Plain, South Georgia.

Allardyce Range and Mount Paget, South Georgia.

The mighty berg – tabular iceberg off South Georgia.

Elephant Island, from where Shackleton and five companions sailed 800 miles to South Georgia.

Icebergs come in a multitude of shapes, sizes and colours. Blue ice.

Iceberg arch, Joinville Island.

Desolate Deception Island. Abandoned water supply boat.

Abandoned base, Almirante Brown in Paradise Harbour.

Seals basking on ice foes in Neko Harbour.

A little living history! The lady in green is Robyn Hurley, the daughter of Frank Hurley, the photographer on Shackleton's Endurance expedition.

Ice sculpture – like a ship's prow. Iceberg in Paradise Harbour.

Farewell to Antarctica, sunset over Brabant Island.

Greenhouse gas	Chemical formula	How and where they are produced
Carbon dioxide	CO_2	• By burning of all forms of fuel: oil, coal, wood, peat and gas. • By respiration in all living organisms • By bacterial decay of living organisms
Methane	CH_4	• From bacterial activity in intestines of cattle and other • living organisms • From decay of rotting vegetation • Natural gas escaping from melting permafrost
Chlorofluorocarbons (CFCs)	CCl_3F CCl_2F_2	• Industrial production for use in aerosols and • refrigerators. E.g. Freons made by DuPont
Nitrous oxide	N_2O	• Decomposition of humus • Burning fossil fuels
Water vapour	H_2O	• Burning of any fossil fuel and plant matter • Respiration in all living organisms • Evaporation from oceans, lakes, rivers

Climate change and natural cycles

Climate changes can be caused by natural cycles. An example of these is the variations in the earth's axis of rotation, and eccentricity in its orbit around the sun known as Milankovitch Cyles as shown in the diagrams below. These alter the amount of solar radiation reaching the earth and where it falls on the surface.

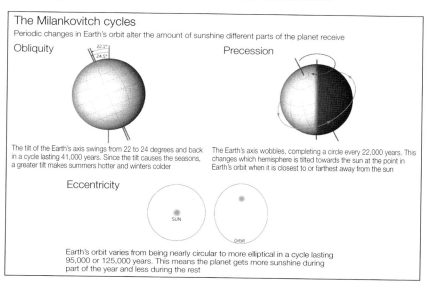

The Milankovitch cycles

Periodic changes in Earth's orbit alter the amount of sunshine different parts of the planet receive

Obliquity

Precession

The tilt of the Earth's axis swings from 22 to 24 degrees and back in a cycle lasting 41,000 years. Since the tilt causes the seasons, a greater tilt makes summers hotter and winters colder

The Earth's axis wobbles, completing a circle every 22,000 years. This changes which hemisphere is tilted towards the sun at the point in Earth's orbit when it is closest to or farthest away from the sun

Eccentricity

SUN

Orbit

Earth's orbit varies from being nearly circular to more elliptical in a cycle lasting 95,000 or 125,000 years. This means the planet gets more sunshine during part of the year and less during the rest

Examples of climatic variation

	Name of period	Duration (millions of years)	Climatic features
Long term	Carboniferous Include Coal Measures	65	Hot and moist, during which thick dense vegetation grew and decayed, forming coal measures
	Jurassic	60	Very warm, a vast range of plants and animals, many large dinosaur fossils remain from this period
	Quaternary	2	Glacial and interglacial periods. Ice caps formed during glacial periods, reaching as far south as the Thames valley
		Duration (hundreds of years)	
Medium term	Medieval Warming period	Approx 400	The Vikings discovered and settled in Greenland and Iceland. Vines grew in England as far north as Yorkshire
	Little Ice Age seventeenth century		Long cold winters in northern Europe. Frost fairs on the Thames. Volcanic activity in Iceland a possible cause
		Duration (years) approx	
Short term	1950s – mid 1960s	13	Cold winters, warm summers
	Mid 1960s – 1980s	18	Warmer winters, cooler summers
	Mid 1980s – 2005	20	Mild winters, some hot summers
	2006 – 2010	4	Colder winters and cooler summers

Solar radiation and its effects

Types of Radiation	Wavelength	Destiny of Radiation
Ultraviolet	10 nm to 400 nm	Most is absorbed by reactions between oxygen and ozone, so most uUV is filtered out of the atmosphere
Visible light	400 nm to 700 nm	Red and blue light are absorbed by plants through photosynthesis; green is not, and is reflected, so plants appear green
Heat energy		Passes through atmosphere and heats surface of earth. Some is then radiated back away from earth surface as longer wavelength radiation i.e., infra-red
Infra-red	0.7 to 1000 μm	Some passes through atmosphere into space, but more is absorbed by gases in the troposphere thus trapping it and warming the planet. This trapping of heat is called the 'greenhouse effect'.

Other factors that can alter solar radiation on earth

There are several other natural factors that can affect the amount of solar radiation received on earth. These are sunspots, solar radiation, interstellar dust clouds, and volcanic ash and dust.

Sunspots

Sunspots are cooler areas of the sun's surface, linked to magnetic changes. However, while the sunspots are cooler areas, the areas around them become hotter. They often occur in 11-year cycles, and they can cause a very small increase in heat received on earth. Sunspots indicate a more active sun. So, when there are fewer of them, less energy reaches the earth. This was observed by Edward Maunder, an English astronomer. He discovered that, approximately between 1650 and 1715, there were very few sunspots and this period coincided with a cool period in northern Europe called the 'Little Ice Age' or 'Maunder minimum'. Glaciers in Europe advanced and some winters were cold enough to hold 'frost fairs' on the frozen Thames, the first in 1607, the last in 1814.

Currently, we are in a 'sunspot minimum', which is due to end in 2013. Despite this sunspot minimum, the temperature of earth's atmosphere has continued to rise slowly.

Interstellar dust clouds

Interstellar dust would reduce solar radiation, but at present we do not seem to have very much scientific evidence to prove this.

Solar Radiation: the sun's brightness

Scientists began to measure the sun's brightness in 1977. Its brightness rose between 1977 and 1985, but has been falling since, but despite this, global temperatures continue to rise slowly.

Volcanic ash and dust clouds

In April 2010, thousands of people, flying with various airlines in Europe and North America, were inconvenienced by the eruption of the Eyafjallajökull volcano in Iceland, but this inconvenience was nothing compared to what happened in Iceland in June 1783. The traveller James Nicol wrote 'numerous pillars of smoke were noticed rising in the fills to the north, fire spouts were observed in the mountains, accompanied by earthquakes.' The Laki volcano had erupted and continued to do so for several months. It produced clouds of poisonous gases which killed 9000 people in Iceland, destroyed half the country's livestock and killed huge areas of vegetation. It created a vast area of cold fog that spread across much of Europe and North America, causing the coldest summer for 500 years, blotting out the sun's radiation, together with downpours and terrible thunderstorms. Crops failed and famine and starvation were widespread both in Europe and North America. 1783 was known as the 'year without summer', and was followed by a bitter winter in which an estimated 23,000 people died in Britain!

So, massive eruptions in the past have caused climate changes. So far, neither Laki, nor another volcano near Eyfjallajökull called Katla have erupted since 1823. Let us hope that they remain dormant. However recent reports from the Iceland metrological service indicates increased seismic activity in the Grímsvötn area in early November 2010. Grímsvötn erupted at the end of September 1996 causing a massive glacial outburst, i.e. flood water under the ice cap which broke through the ice, flooding the large area of land called Skeiðará sandur to the south, sweeping away electric cables, bridges and large sections of the road.

Reasons for concern about global warning
Scientists the world over are very concerned. Although such natural cycles and other phenomena described above may account for some change, human (anthropogenic) activities, such as electricity production, transport, cattle-rearing, and even human respiration, are all pumping more and more heat and carbon dioxide into the atmosphere — about 28 billion tons of CO_2 annually. So, these activities are all contributing to heat retention in the atmosphere. At the same time, huge areas of forests which absorb and reduce CO_2 levels in the air are being cut down. Also, as the oceans warm up, they too can absorb less CO_2, thus more goes into the atmosphere, and the levels are approaching 400 parts per million now, higher than at any time in earth's recorded history.

So what are the effects of all this on polar regions? In the Arctic, reports generally indicate glacial retreat (notably in Greenland), earlier spring thaws and later refreezing of the sea ice cap surrounding the North Pole, together with considerable thinning of the sea ice and its retreat towards the North Pole. The sad picture opposite illustrates one effect of this.

Independent Newspapers

Walrus hiding on an ice floe in the arctic

Some scientists now predict the total disappearance of summer sea ice by the end of this century, or earlier.

There could be several effects of this. The Arctic Ocean will warm up. Warmer seas absorb less oxygen, so fewer fish, at all levels of the food chain, will survive, with a knock-on effect on seals, whales and polar bears. Polar bears and walruses cannot swim far, so therefore need the ice to move around on, to hunt seals, so if it disappears, their territory will shrink, leading to starvation and death. The photograph of the walruses speaks for itself.

The disappearance of summer sea ice will have little or no effect on sea levels, because it is just floating on water, but the ice cap acts as one of the earth's 'air conditioners', providing cool air to reduce temperatures over hot continents — remember the terrible heat wave in Moscow in August 2010, and the subsequent forest fires? The cool air helps redistribute atmospheric heat by causing storms and wind and rain (which is needed for agriculture), and these storms may move farther north, away from the wheat-growing areas, leading to crop failure.

Loss of all Arctic sea ice will lead to much easier exploitation of the Arctic, for oil and gas, which in turn will lead to the release of much more CO_2 and further heating — a trend already being seen.

The worst possible effect, of course, would be the complete collapse and melt down of the Greenland ice sheet, which is two miles thick in places. It has been estimated that if it melted away, sea levels worldwide would rise by 11 metres (over 30 feet)! Imagine the effect on many of our major coastal cities, and vast areas of low lying coast; it would be a catastrophe.

Temperatures in Antarctica appear to be rising, and glaciers are in retreat, especially in the Antarctic Peninsula. Plants and animals usually found further north are slowing spreading southwards.

A number of vast icebergs have recently broken off some of the major ice shelves, as occurred in 2002, when the Larsen B ice shelf broke up. This kind of break up of the floating ice sheet could in turn allow glaciers previously held back by the ice sheet to flow much more rapidly into the sea and melt, thus helping to raise sea levels. The following photographs illustrate this break up.

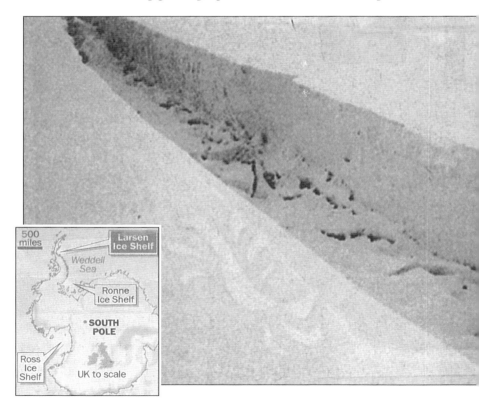

It has been estimated that if the entire Antarctic ice sheet were to melt, the sea levels world-wide could rise by around a 100 metres!

Reasons for scepticism

Does the man or woman in the street really care about this? 'Not yet,' seems to be the answer, since several events have recently conspired to increase public scepticism about global warming. Many people will recall the uproar over some e-mails stolen from the University of East Anglia's Climate Research Unit when accusations were made that some scientists had been manipulating and concealing data. It appears however that there is actually no evidence that data was being systematically falsified or dishonestly manipulated in referred journals. But the event did increase public scepticism about global warming.

Then came a statement by the head of the IPCC (International Panel on Climate Change) that all Himalayan glaciers would disappear within 30 years. This is very unlikely to happen. The public is also bombarded with continuous reports of 'doom and gloom' if nothing is done to ameliorate global warming. This is unfortunate because crying wolf too often will induce public boredom, when in fact the situation could be becoming serious. Added to this, the winter 2009–2010 was the coldest for 31 years over northern Europe, followed in December 2010 by one of the coldest recorded Decembers. So inevitably people were asking 'what happened to global warming?'

The problem is that events such as these make for easy headlines. However, statements such as 'a global warming trend of 0.15–0.20°C per decade' or 'CO_2 levels in the atmosphere have risen from above 280 ppmv (parts per million by volume) to nearly 390 ppmv today', both of which are true statements, do not!

Scientists need to be aware of public reaction to scary statements about climate change, while at the same time trying to convince the public to support measures that will reduce the output of greenhouse gases. There are many ways of doing this and I do not propose to list them all here since everyone is aware of the need to use less energy, and we can all do our bit to that end.

What caused the ice ages and why did they end so quickly?
There are many theories about the causes of ice ages, from interstellar dust clouds blocking out sunlight, volcanic dust, to the effects of the Milankovitch cycles. These are all possible, and research continues, but new evidence from Chinese cave records show that monsoons failed during all the last four ice-age terminations. The reason, long suspected, is that melting of the ice sheets alters ocean circulation, producing drastic changes in regional climates. So it appears that ice ages basically were caused by a combination of reduction of summer sunshine, causing ice and snow that fell in winter to not melt fully, and by decreasing CO_2 levels in the air.

What caused the ice sheets to melt and thus the ice ages to end? It seems that ice sheets accumulate until they become almost unstable, and at this point a small increase in summer sunshine can

New Scientist magazine

initiate large-scale melting. This releases fresh water into the oceans, thereby reducing ocean circulation and so less heat is carried north, allowing the southern oceans to warm and release CO_2, which warms the whole planet, leading to further melting and more CO_2 release. This is an example of positive feedback. The diagram on page 74 illustrates this:

Where are we today relative to the ice ages and the present situation in the polar regions? The great ice sheets covering Europe and North America and Russia have long gone; smaller ice caps such as the Vatnajökull in Iceland, and the larger Greenland ice cap are merely the remnants of these vast ice sheets. As CO_2 levels in the atmosphere rise, it is reckoned that they could cause 'runaway warming' which could cause rapid meltdown of the remaining Greenland ice sheet and as previously mentioned, an 11 metre (about 33 feet) global sea level rise.

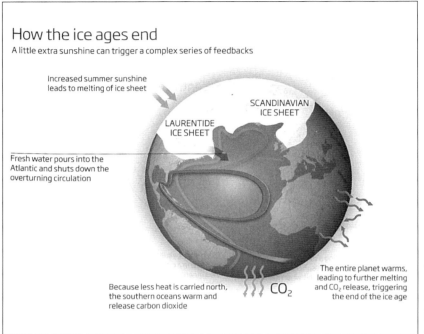

How the ice ages end

A little extra sunshine can trigger a complex series of feedbacks

Increased summer sunshine leads to melting of ice sheet

SCANDINAVIAN ICE SHEET

LAURENTIDE ICE SHEET

Fresh water pours into the Atlantic and shuts down the overturning circulation

The entire planet warms, leading to further melting and CO_2 release, triggering the end of the ice age

Because less heat is carried north, the southern oceans warm and release carbon dioxide

CO_2

New Scientist magazine

To illustrate the positive feedback effect, we need to remember that snow and ice reflect sunshine. When they melt, trees, water, soil and rocks become exposed to the sunshine and absorb its heat. This in turn warms the air more, thus melting more snow and ice which leads to more warming and melting. The whole cycle is self-perpetuating, and self-fuelling.

Another example is the release of methane, a potent greenhouse gas, from the melting Arctic permafrost. As the permafrost in the tundra melts, methane is released and in 2005 methane was found bubbling up in western Siberian lakes. Siberian bogs are reckoned to contain a quarter of the methane in the world's land surface. Its release will retain more heat in the atmosphere, leading to more permafrost melting and more methane release, and thus more global warming.

In Greenland the ice cap is now threatened in two ways. Firstly, meltwater on the surface runs down into the crevasses, lubricates the ice cap base and thus allows the ice to slide into the sea more quickly. Secondly, as the ice cap slowly lowers, it is exposed to warmer air, which can speed up its melting.

All these possibilities do seem quite threatening and there is a potential for disaster, but man is an intelligent and clever creature. One wonders however, if we are wise enough to take action to prevent these possible disasters before it is too late. Personally, I work on the precautionary principle. It is very difficult to prove that human activities are causing global warning and climate change, but if we assume that they are, then we can and should take action to reduce these activities. There are two advantages to this approach, the first being that by reducing energy consumption and greenhouse gas emissions, we will begin to cool the planet down and slowly, hopefully, prevent the worst predictions of sea level rises from coming true.

Finale, or The Last Word
The following article by Charles Emerson entitled 'Our friends in the North' is taken from the *Independent* newspaper in October 2010, neatly summarises the developing situation in the Arctic Ocean.

OUR FRIENDS IN THE NORTH

ECOLOGY!

'In the Norwegian town of Kirkenes — a few degrees above the Arctic Circle and a few miles from the Russian border — older inhabitants still remember the revving of Soviet tank engines during military exercises during the Cold War. The Kola Peninsula, to the east, was one of the most militarised regions on earth; the Barents Sea, to the north, was a bastion for the Soviet nuclear submarine fleet. The maritime border between the Soviet Union and Norway was disputed — with a huge overlap between both sides' claims — and remained so after the collapse of the USSR in 1991.

'In April this year, President Medvedev made a two-day state visit to Oslo. After years of on-off negotiations, Russia and Norway finally reached a preliminary deal to split the difference in the Barents Sea. The main reason? Oil and gas. Both countries need to exploit the resources of the Arctic if they are to boost — or even maintain — levels of oil and gas production on which the rest of Europe (including the UK) may increasingly depend.

'As Norway's North Sea production reaches its limits, and as Russia's Siberian fields are pumped dry, both countries have turned north. (According to BP, Russian gas production declined 12pc in 2009, through this partly reflects changes in demand.) An agreement on the Norwegian–Russian maritime border opens the way for investment in offshore development, which would have otherwise been commercially unthinkable.

'The global economic crisis has put some developments on hold, as finances have become tighter, gas prices have fallen and uncertainty about the global economy has increased. The date for the opening of the massive Russian Shtokman natural gas field — the first phase of which is a joint venture between Gazprom, Norway's Statoil and France's Total — has been pushed back three years, to 2016.

'The outlook for large-scale liquefied natural gas exports to the United States has dimmed since the American shale-gas boom of recent years — though that may not matter if alternative buyers are found in China. State-owned shipping company Sovocomflot sent an experimental shipment of gas condensate through the Russian North-East Passage this summer. It is here — rather than along the totemic North-West Passage — that development is likely to be focussed in the coming years. The Gulf of Mexico spill has been seen by many to symbolise the hubris of the global hydrocarbon industry in pushing into more and more environmentally challenging parts of the world. In the US, public anger at apparent regulatory oversights, and a cowboy culture within the operators of the Deepwater Horizon rig, has led to a backlash against oil companies in general. According to the *Los Angeles Times*, support for offshore drilling in the US Arctic has fallen from 58pc to 46pc. Rightly, US interior secretary Ken Salazar has announced that Arctic drilling will be delayed pending further assessments.

'What impact, if any, the Gulf spill has on the long-term prospects for development in the Norwegian or Russian Arctic is unclear. Already stringent environmental frameworks in Norway will probably be tightened; gold plating will, inevitably become the norm.

'In Russia, environmental concerns are unlikely to change the government's strategic attitude towards oil and gas development in the Arctic, nor the views of Russian main players (Rosneft, Gazprom, Lukoil); nor the attitudes of thousands of Russians who live in the Arctic, and who are hoping for a hydrocarbon boom. The technology-rich Western partners that Russia needs to develop offshore fields may become marginally more wary of putting their reputations on the line in the Russian Arctic. But, rightly or wrongly, if the price and policies are correct, such obstacles will probably be overcome.

'There is room for contract and competition here. There is certainly the risk of environmental disaster. There is also room for co-operation. Just as between Norway and Russia, the possibility of future oil and gas wealth may help push Canada and the United States towards the resolution of an outstanding dispute in the Beaufort Sea.

'Governments should try, a much as possible, to develop common protocols on environmental protection and clean-up, because the issue of Arctic oil and gas development — in

Russia and elsewhere — is not going to go away any time soon.

(Charles Emmerson is a London-based independent writer and adviser, and the author of *The Future History of the Arctic* (Random House, 2010).

Mike Palmer, October 2010

Bibliography

The following books and documents have been consulted during the writing of this book

Aeberhard, D., Benson, A. & Phillips, L., *Rough guide to Argentina*, 2000. Rough Guides Limited, London.

Blake, Joe, *Restoring the Great Britain*, 1989. Redcliffe Press Limited, Bristol.

Box, Ben, *South American Handbook*, 2010. Footprint Books.

Brooks, J.R.V., *Penguin Dictionary of Geology*, 1972. Penguin Books Limited, London

Bruges, James, *The Big Earth Book, Ideas and solutions for a planet in crisis*, 2008. Alastair Sawday Publishing, Bristol

Cawkell, Mary, *The Falkland Story*, 1983. Anthony Nelson, Shropshire

Hart, Ian, *Pesca: the history of Compañia Argentina de Pesca Sociedad Anómina of Buenos Aires. An account of the pioneer modern whaling and sealing company in the Antarctic.* Rev ed 2002, Aiden Ellis, Salcombe

Independent Newspaper, photo 'walrus woes', article Our friends in the north.

McIntosh, E.& Walton, D.W.H., *Environmental Management Plan for South Georgia*, British Antarctic Survey

Miles, Hugh & Salisbury, Mike, *Kingdom of the Ice Bear. A portrait of the Arctic.* 1985. BBC, London.

New Scientist magazine, extracts from 'Secrets of the ice ages' and photo may 22nd 2010 of melting on the Greenland icecap.

Pretor-Pinney, Gavin, *The Cloudspotter's Guide*, 2006. Hodder & Stoughton Limited, London

Stone, Tony, *Images*, 2000. Phillips School Atlas, Chancellor Press

Tarrant, Chris, *Tarrant on Top of the World*, 2005. Weidenfeld & Nicholson, London

The Editors, *Insight Guides: Iceland*, 2000. Insight Guides, London

The Times, Larsen B ice shelf, photo by Steve Morgan, Greenpeace.

Wagstaff, William, *The Falkland Islands*, 2001. Chalfont St.Peter, Bradt Travel Guides Limited

Webb, Peter, *Ice Bears and Kotick*, 2007. Seafarer Books

Wyatt, Richard, The less famous rescue plan for *SS Great Britain*, *Western Daily Press*, 16 November 2010.